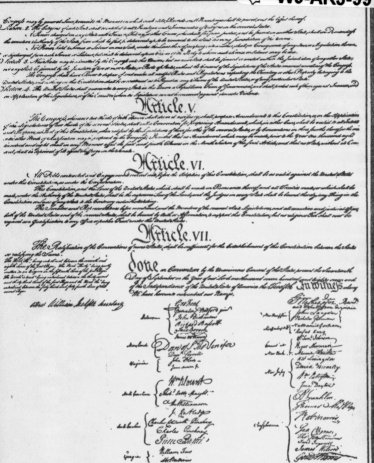

# UNITED STATES OF AMERICA

# YOUR RUGGED

BRUCE ALLYN FINDLAY

ESTHER BLAIR FINDLAY

*Illustrations by*

RICHARD DAWSON

AMERICAN IDEALS SERIES • • • •

# ONSTITUTION

*How America's House of Freedom*
*Is Planned and Built*

STANFORD UNIVERSITY PRESS

## ACKNOWLEDGMENTS

For invaluable criticisms, comments, and suggestions, the authors wish to thank Elizabeth Solem Dutton, Eugene Harley, Richard Dawson, Paul R. Murray, James Mussatti, Paul Cox, George Wakefield, Ray Brown, Edria Wallis, John C. Almack, A. John Bartky, Harry William Porter, Gordon B. and Allan H. Crary, and the staff of Stanford University Press.

# CONTENTS

THE PREAMBLE
TO THE CONSTITUTION    1

THE ARTICLES
AND THE AMENDMENTS:

# THE PREAMBLE TO THE CONSTITUTION

## PURPOSES FOR WHICH THE CONSTITUTION WAS WRITTEN

# Preamble

"WE, THE PEOPLE OF THE UNITED STATES, IN ORDER TO FORM A MORE PERFECT UNION, ESTABLISH JUSTICE, INSURE DOMESTIC TRANQUILITY, PROVIDE FOR THE COMMON DEFENSE, PROMOTE THE GENERAL WELFARE, AND SECURE THE BLESSINGS OF LIBERTY TO OURSELVES AND OUR POSTERITY, DO ORDAIN AND ESTABLISH THIS CONSTITUTION FOR THE UNITED STATES OF AMERICA."

In Witness Whereof:
WE SET OUR HANDS AND SEALS.

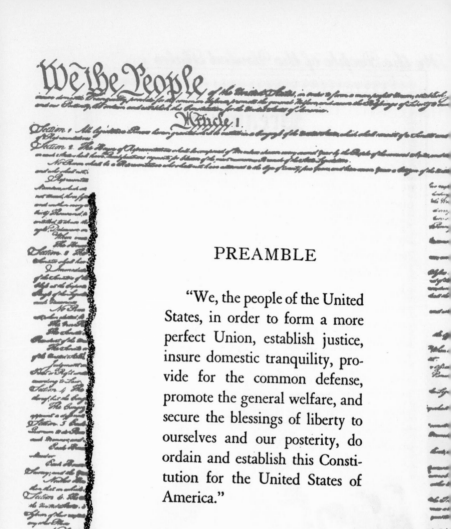

## PREAMBLE

"We, the people of the United States, in order to form a more perfect Union, establish justice, insure domestic tranquility, provide for the common defense, promote the general welfare, and secure the blessings of liberty to ourselves and our posterity, do ordain and establish this Constitution for the United States of America."

# We the People of the United States ...

## DO ORDAIN AND ESTABLISH
## THIS CONSTITUTION FOR THE UNITED STATES
## OF AMERICA

Those words are very important to you and to all other citizens of the United States. In many countries, governments are not run by all of the people, but by small groups of people for their own selfish purposes. In the famous Preamble to our Constitution, *We the People of the United States* proclaim to the world that our government *belongs to* the people, is *run by* the people, and *exists for the good of* the people.

In Washington, D.C., the original handwritten copy of our Constitution is kept on display. But remember that the Constitution is not just a historical document. It is a plan of government that is working today even better than when it was written. It is yours to know, to use, to respect, and if necessary to defend. For you are one of "the People of the United States."

## TO FORM A MORE PERFECT UNION

Our country won its independence from Great Britain in the year 1781. For eight years after that, this country was governed under a constitution called the Articles of Confederation. But there were faults in the Articles. The United States of America, in spite of its name, was far from being a "perfect Union." It was instead, as the Articles said, a "league of friendship" among the states.

In time, some of the states became less friendly toward one another. Soon they began to quarrel seriously. Instead of pulling together as a team, the states were pulling in different directions. There was danger that the states might break away and become small separate countries.

The nation's leaders feared that our new country might fail. For this reason they called a convention of citizens from the various states to meet and study these problems. This group of citizens, now called the Constitutional Con-

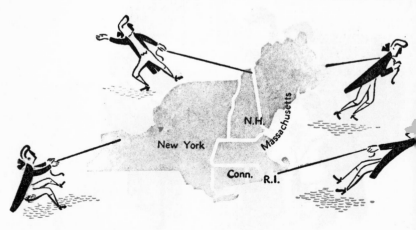

vention, began its meetings in May 1787 at Independence Hall in Philadelphia. All the men were leaders in their states. Among them were such famous citizens as George Washington, Benjamin Franklin, and James Madison.

For a while the delegates to the Convention tried to patch up the Articles of Confederation and make them work. But they soon decided to make an entirely new plan of Government in order to form "a more perfect Union." On September 17, 1787, they put their plan into final form and signed it. They had written the Constitution of the United States of America— the plan for our government.

We today are proud to be citizens of a single strong nation. Our nation is respected by foreign countries and is prosperous at home. Our farm products and manufactured goods pass freely from state to state. We ourselves can go easily across state boundaries without having to carry passports. These are a few of the benefits we enjoy because "a more perfect Union" was established under our Constitution.

## TO ESTABLISH JUSTICE

Our Constitution tells how our laws are to be passed and how our courts are to be run so that every citizen will get the same fair treatment from the government. Laws and punishments are the same for everyone.

When the Constitution was written, there were injustices in the world that would seem strange to us today. In some countries, for example, nobles were tried in their own special courts under special laws. Kings sometimes ordered people to be executed without a trial. As you will see, the men who wrote our Constitution took care that injustices like these should not be allowed in the United States.

But more than that, these farsighted men gave us a system of laws and courts that protects us from newer kinds of injustice. In some countries today, governments give people unfair trials in order to rob them of their property, to sentence them to slave labor camps, or even to execute them. But "We the People of the United States" have ordered that there shall be no unfair trials or unfair punishments in this country. Every American citizen enjoys "equal justice under law."

## *We the People of the United States, in Order . . .*

### TO INSURE DOMESTIC TRANQUILITY

Before the Constitution was adopted, the United States government had little power to help keep the country peaceful and orderly. After the War for Independence, times were hard. Here and there, some people rebelled against their state governments, and the national government lacked power to help the states. Nor did the government have power to settle disputes between the states, even when these disputes threatened to turn into real warfare.

The Constitution settled such problems as these and has protected our "domestic tranquility" ever since. People now can live without fear of violence. When disagreements arise between states, the states let the national government settle their disagreements justly. If a rebellion should occur, the government has the power to step in and enforce the laws of the country and protect the lives and property of the people.

# We the People of the United States, in Order ...

## TO PROVIDE FOR THE COMMON DEFENSE

Our government must do more than keep things peaceful at home. It must also be strong enough to keep enemy nations from conquering this land and taking away our property and lives. There are several clauses in the Constitution that allow our government to take care of the country's changing needs for an army and navy to protect us against a foreign attack.

The United States loves peace and works within the United Nations and in many other ways to keep peace in the world. But we have the strength to fight hard against our enemies, whether they threaten all the states or only one of them. This is called "the common defense." Partly because our Constitution has wise plans for the common defense, our country has never lost a war in all its history.

## TO PROMOTE THE GENERAL WELFARE

This phrase states one of the most important ideals of the American people.

When we speak of a person's welfare we mean his health, happiness, and prosperity. "The general welfare" means the health, happiness, and prosperity of everyone. When neighbors help neighbors, they are promoting the general welfare. When private citizens and organizations carry out campaigns and spend huge sums of money helping others, they too are promoting the general welfare.

The makers of the Constitution planned for the government also to promote the general welfare. But they ordered the government to do things that would benefit everyone, and not to help any one person or group of persons at the expense of all the rest—as many foreign governments had done and some still do.

Our national government employs many persons to promote the general welfare. Some workers look after our soil, minerals, forests, and national parks. Others help farmers, manufacturers, and merchants do their jobs better. Still other government employees work to prevent floods, accidents, and the spread of disease.

## TO SECURE THE BLESSINGS OF LIBERTY
## TO OURSELVES AND OUR POSTERITY

In 1787, the English colonies in America had already won their liberty and had been states for several years. But Washington, Franklin, Madison, and the others at the Constitutional Convention wished to preserve this liberty so that their posterity—the future generations of Americans—might have liberty too. The Constitution they wrote helps to preserve two kinds of liberty for all of us. First is the liberty of the country, protected against control by foreign countries. Second is the liberty of Americans, guarded from being ruled over unjustly by other Americans who might try to seize the government.

The liberty we enjoy does not make any of us free to do whatever he wants to do whenever he wants to do it. Our liberty does not give us the right to take away the lives and property of others. If that were allowed, one man's liberty would mean another man's loss of liberty. Like justice, liberty must be equal for everybody.

# We the People of the United States . . .

## DO ORDAIN AND ESTABLISH THIS CONSTITUTION FOR THE UNITED STATES OF AMERICA

Within a year after the Constitution was written, most of the states decided to ratify or approve it. In April 1789, George Washington became the first President, and the actual building of the new government began.

Under the Articles of Confederation, most of the powers of government belonged to the states and few belonged to the national government. But under the Constitution the powers are more equally divided between state governments and the national government. This system gives our country a *federal* government.

When a government or any part of it grows too powerful, it may try to take away the people's rights. To meet this danger, the Constitution calls for a *separation of powers*. That is, the national government has three distinct branches, each with its own separate powers and duties. Each branch helps to keep the other two from doing unwise or unjust things. This arrangement is called a "system of checks and balances," because each branch helps to check and balance the powers of the other two branches. The three branches are: (1) the legislative branch, which makes the laws; (2) the executive branch, which carries out the laws; and (3) the judicial branch, which tries cases in court and explains the meanings of the laws.

The Constitution tells what actions may be

taken by the national government and by the state governments. It makes the rules for electing citizens to serve in the national government. It tells what kinds of laws may be made for the nation, how they are to be made, and how they are to be enforced.

After more than one hundred and sixty years, there is still no sign that this rugged Constitution of ours will ever wear out. The United States, once small and weak, has become a large and mighty nation. And, more important than its size and strength, our country is a land of freedom and justice.

In the following pages of this book, you will find the words of the Constitution printed part by part, with explanations of their meaning and importance. You will see how wisely and well the men at the Constitutional Convention did their work for the benefit of all the other Americans coming after them. By understanding the Constitution, you can help to keep it rugged in all the years ahead.

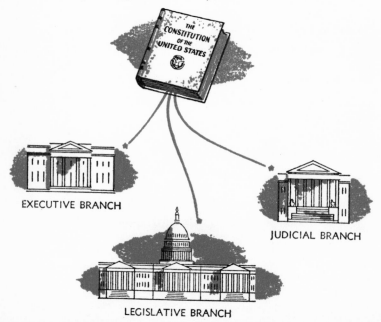

EXECUTIVE BRANCH

JUDICIAL BRANCH

LEGISLATIVE BRANCH

# ARTICLE
## I

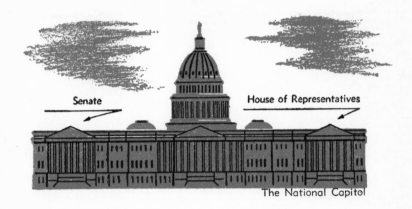

Senate       House of Representatives

The National Capitol

## THE LEGISLATIVE BRANCH
## MAKES THE LAWS

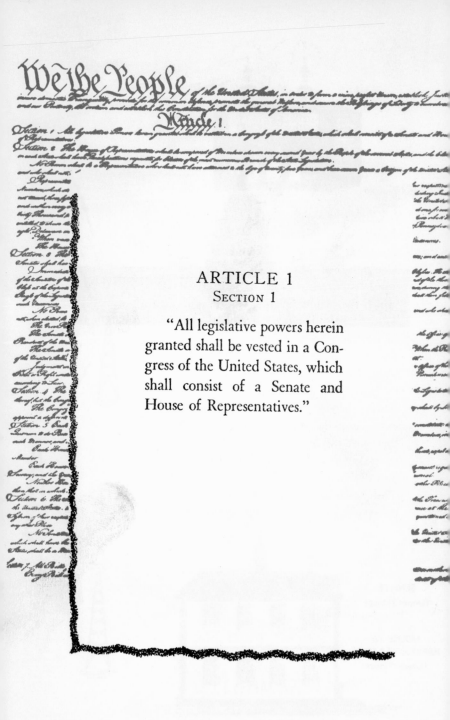

# ARTICLE 1
## SECTION 1

"All legislative powers herein granted shall be vested in a Congress of the United States, which shall consist of a Senate and House of Representatives."

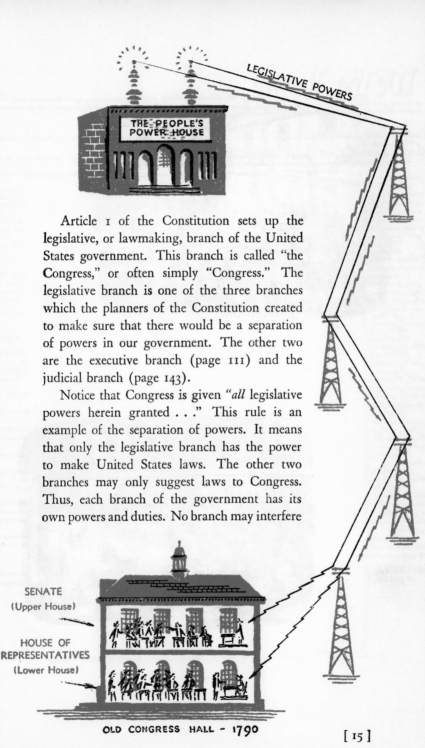

LEGISLATIVE POWERS

THE PEOPLE'S POWER HOUSE

Article 1 of the Constitution sets up the legislative, or lawmaking, branch of the United States government. This branch is called "the Congress," or often simply "Congress." The legislative branch is one of the three branches which the planners of the Constitution created to make sure that there would be a separation of powers in our government. The other two are the executive branch (page 111) and the judicial branch (page 143).

Notice that Congress is given *"all* legislative powers herein granted . . ." This rule is an example of the separation of powers. It means that only the legislative branch has the power to make United States laws. The other two branches may only suggest laws to Congress. Thus, each branch of the government has its own powers and duties. No branch may interfere

SENATE
(Upper House)

HOUSE OF
REPRESENTATIVES
(Lower House)

OLD CONGRESS HALL - 1790

[ 15 ]

THE SENATE

THE HOUSE OF REPRESENTATIVES

with the powers and duties of other branches, except in ways the Constitution allows.

The power to make the nation's laws actually belongs to the American people, but the people have given Congress the right to make these laws for them. But even Congress is allowed to make only those kinds of laws which the Constitution says Congress may make.

The United States is so large and has so many millions of citizens that all of them could not possibly travel to one place and vote on the nation's laws. Instead, these citizens elect between 500 and 600 citizens to go to Washington, D.C., to serve as Senators and members of the House of Representatives. Each Senator and each member of the House *represents* the many citizens of his state or his district. That is, while he is in Congress he speaks and votes in the place of those citizens, and acts for them in other ways. Because the government is run by elected representatives of the people, it is called a *representative* government.

*You give:* (*a*) Power only to Congress to make laws for the nation; (*b*) instructions that there shall always be two separate divisions in Congress.

*You get:* (*a*) Laws which have been carefully thought out by members of Congress elected to represent you; (*b*) control of members of Congress, since you vote them into office and can vote them out again; (*c*) two divisions, or "houses," of Congress, each of which guards the nation against mistakes made by the other.

# ARTICLE 1
## Section 2
### Clause 1

"The House of Representatives shall be composed of members chosen every second year by the people of the several states, and the electors in each state shall have the qualifications requisite for electors of the most numerous branch of the State Legislature."

### Clause 2

"No person shall be a Representative who shall not have attained to the age of twenty-five years, and been seven years a citizen of the United States, and who shall not, when elected, be an inhabitant of that state in which he shall be chosen."

In this country, which has a representative government, deciding who shall be permitted to vote in the various elections is important. The makers of the Constitution could not agree on who should be allowed to vote for members of the House of Representatives. They settled the argument by letting each state make its own rules for electing Representatives. But the Constitution did order that anyone should be allowed to vote for a Representative if he was allowed in his own state to vote for members of "the most numerous branch of the State Legislature." In most states, the branch of the Legislature with more members was also the branch elected by more of the people.

As another way to make the House of Representatives respect the wishes of the people, the Constitution ordered that Representatives must be elected every two years.

Your Representative Must Be:—

1. At least twenty-five years old.

2. A citizen of the United States for at least seven years.

3. A resident of the state in which he is elected.

*You give:* Permission to citizens of your state to represent you in the House of Representatives if (*a*) they can meet requirements of age, citizenship, and residence; and (*b*) they can win an election.

*You get:* (*a*) Representatives, both old and young, who have been citizens of the United States long enough to know its needs, and who know the wishes of the people in their own states; (*b*) a chance every two years either to re-elect your Representatives or to elect new ones.

# ARTICLE 1
## Section 2
### Clause 3

"Representatives and direct taxes shall be apportioned among the several states which may be included within this Union, according to their respective numbers, which shall be determined by adding to the whole number of free persons, including those bound to service for a term of years, and excluding Indians not taxed, three fifths of all other persons. The actual enumeration shall be made within three years after the first meeting of the Congress of the United States, and within every subsequent term of ten years, in such manner as they shall by law direct. The number of Representatives shall not exceed one for every thirty thousand, but each state shall have at least one Representative; and until such enumeration shall be made, the state of New Hampshire shall be entitled to choose 3; Massachusetts, 8; Rhode Island and Providence Plantations, 1; Connecticut, 5; New York, 6; New Jersey, 4; Pennsylvania, 8; Delaware, 1; Maryland, 6; Virginia, 10; North Carolina, 5; South Carolina, 5; and Georgia, 3."

Some parts of the Constitution are no longer in effect. In this book, these parts are marked out by light lines.

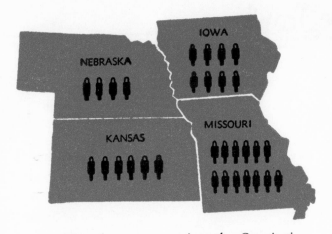

This clause was put into the Constitution as a result of the "Great Compromise" of the Constitutional Convention. Delegates from the larger states, led by Virginia, wanted the total number of members of Congress to be divided among the states according to their populations. That is, they wanted a state with twice as many people as another state to have twice as many members in Congress. But the delegates from the smaller states, led by New Jersey, wanted every state to have the same number of members.

After long and bitter arguments in the Constitutional Convention, the large states and the small states finally worked out the "Great Compromise." They agreed that the more people any state had, the more members that state could send to the House of Representatives. But they also agreed that each state should send two members, and two only, to the Senate (see page 28).

This compromise satisfied both the larger

and the smaller states. The state with the largest population had the most Representatives in the House. The smallest state, however, had as many members in the Senate as the largest state. And no bill could become a law unless it was passed by both the House and the Senate.

To avoid arguments over the number of Representatives from any state, the Constitution ordered that a census—an official count of the number of people—should be taken in each state every ten years. A national law now requires that after every census each state must be told how many Representatives it may have in Congress.

The men who wrote the Constitution intended that there should be not more than one Representative in Congress for every thirty thousand people. But as the population increased, people saw that the House might have too many members to do its work well. For this reason a law was passed in 1929 limiting the total number of Representatives to 435.* But each state, no matter how small its population, must still have at least one member in the House of Representatives.

In the first part of the clause dealing with Representatives, the Constitution also says that

John Q. Citizen

the payment of direct taxes must be divided among the states in the same way that the total number of Representatives is divided. (Direct taxes are those which individuals pay directly to the government.)

*You give:* (*a*) Rules which make clear that the number of Representatives from each state shall depend on the population of that state; (*b*) instructions that the people are to be counted every ten years.

*You get:* A House of Representatives (*a*) which is elected directly by the people; and (*b*) in which the states with larger populations have more votes than the states with smaller populations.

* If there were one Representative for every 30,000 people, the House of Representatives today would have more than 5,000 members instead of only 435.

# ARTICLE 1
## SECTION 2
### CLAUSE 4

"When vacancies happen in the representation from any state, the executive authority thereof shall issue writs of election to fill such vacancies."

### CLAUSE 5

"The House of Representatives shall choose their Speaker and other officers; and shall have the sole power of impeachment."

According to Clause 4, if a Representative dies or resigns, the governor of his state must order a special state election to fill his vacant seat. This clause keeps any Representative from being appointed by a state governor instead of being elected by the people. But a state governor is allowed to appoint a Senator to fill a vacant seat in the Senate until the voters can elect a Senator (see pages 240–41).

The Speaker of the House of Representatives has a very important position. He is chairman of all meetings of the House. He also has other duties that are stated in the rules of the House. He is the leader of the majority party —that is, of the political party having the largest number of members in the House. And if both the President and the Vice-President of the United States should die, the Speaker would become President (see page 121).

Order of Presidential Succession

*You give:* To the House of Representatives the right to choose its own Speaker and other officers.

*You get:* An able leader of the House who is also prepared to lead the nation if both the President and the Vice-President should die.

The words "sole power of impeachment" in Clause 5 mean that only the House of Representatives has the right to accuse a public official of the United States of some important crime. Such crimes are "treason, bribery, or other high crimes or misdemeanors" (see page 141).

Speaker

Members of the
House of Representatives

Clerk

IMPEACHMENT
CHARGES

When the House has worked out its charges against the official, it brings them before the Senate (see page 39). The House acts as the prosecutor. It is like a district attorney presenting the charges against a man accused of a crime. The Senate acts as the judge and the jury in the case.

*You give:* Responsibility to the House to watch the actions of government officials, and power to accuse them if they are dishonest, or disloyal to their country.

*You get:* Protection against dishonesty and other criminal actions by government officials.

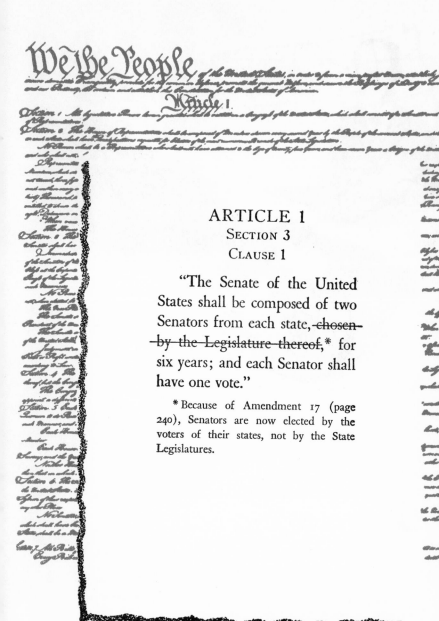

# ARTICLE 1
## SECTION 3
### CLAUSE 1

"The Senate of the United States shall be composed of two Senators from each state, ~~chosen by the Legislature thereof,~~* for six years; and each Senator shall have one vote."

* Because of Amendment 17 (page 240), Senators are now elected by the voters of their states, not by the State Legislatures.

★ ★ Two Senators from each state
elected for six years
One vote for each Senator

This clause is a part of the "Great Compromise" (see page 21). The states with small populations were afraid that the states with large populations might control Congress and pass laws that the smaller states did not like. But this clause removed their fears. Every state, no matter how small, would have two Senators to guard its interests. Senators from the small states could vote together to defeat any unfair bill passed by the House of Representatives, in which the large states had more members.

*You give:* Each state the right to elect two members of the Senate, who serve six-year terms.

*You get:* The same number of Senators for each state. This keeps states or regions with large populations from gaining too much power over states or regions with small populations.

# ARTICLE 1
## Section 3
### Clause 2

"Immediately after they shall be assembled in consequence of the first election, they shall be divided as equally as may be into three classes. ~~The seats of the Senators of the first class shall be vacated at the expiration of the second year, of the second class at the expiration of the fourth year, and of the third class at the expiration of the sixth year,~~ so that one-third may be chosen every second year; and if vacancies happen by resignation, or otherwise, during the recess of the Legislature of any state, the Executive thereof may make temporary appointments until the next meeting of the Legislature, which shall then fill such vacancies."*

* Amendment 17 changes this method of filling vacancies.

The six-year terms of one-third of the Senators end every two years. Then new Senators must be elected to take their places. Two-thirds of the members of the Senate, however, are "carried over." Thus, the Senate is sometimes called "the house that never dies."

*You give:* The people an opportunity to elect one-third of the Senate every two years.

*You get:* A continuing and experienced Senate, yet one in which the actions of one-third of the members are reviewed by the voters every two years.

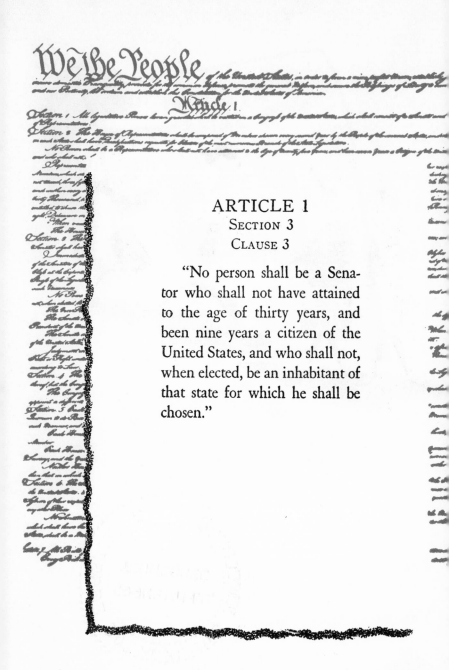

# ARTICLE 1
## SECTION 3
### CLAUSE 3

"No person shall be a Senator who shall not have attained to the age of thirty years, and been nine years a citizen of the United States, and who shall not, when elected, be an inhabitant of that state for which he shall be chosen."

A Senator must be:

1. At least thirty years old.

2. A citizen of the United States for at least nine years.

3. A resident of the state in which he is elected.

*You give:* Requirements for Senators stricter than those for Representatives.

*You get:* Mature, experienced Senators who know the problems of the nation and their states.

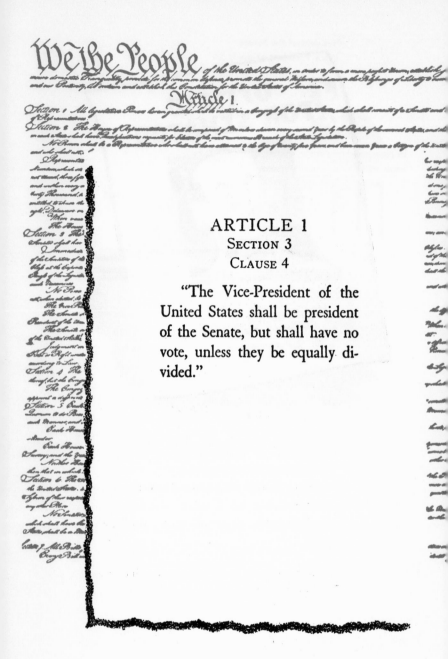

# ARTICLE 1
## Section 3
### Clause 4

"The Vice-President of the United States shall be president of the Senate, but shall have no vote, unless they be equally divided."

President of the Senate
(Vice-President of the U.S.)

"The vote is a tie, Mr. President. How do you vote?"

Clerk

The only duty assigned to the Vice-President by the Constitution is to be the president of the Senate. This duty is important. When there is a tie vote in the Senate, the Vice-President can vote and break the tie. As president of the Senate, he learns about new bills and laws, appointments of important officials, and treaties with other nations. He needs to understand these things in case he should suddenly become President of the United States.

The Vice-President is usually invited to meet with the President's Cabinet. This helps him to know about the plans and actions of the President.

*You give:* The Vice-President an important post as president of the Senate, where he can keep in touch with the problems of the nation.

*You get:* As president of the Senate, a man who has been elected by the people.

[ 35 ]

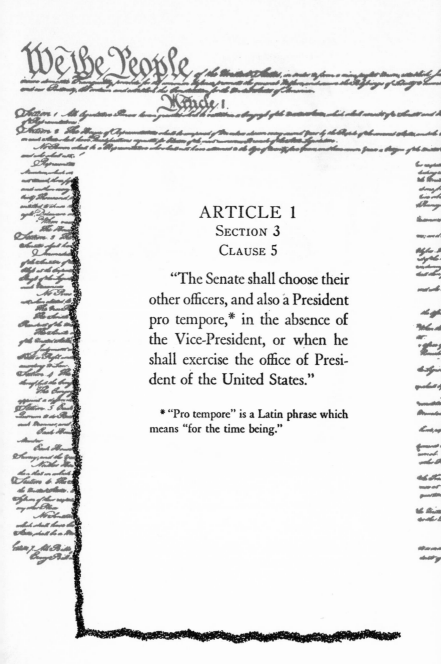

# ARTICLE 1
## SECTION 3
### CLAUSE 5

"The Senate shall choose their other officers, and also a President pro tempore,* in the absence of the Vice-President, or when he shall exercise the office of President of the United States."

\* "Pro tempore" is a Latin phrase which means "for the time being."

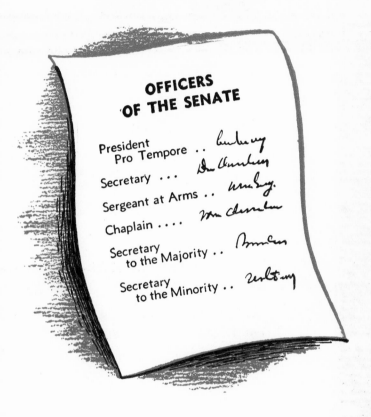

OFFICERS OF THE SENATE

President Pro Tempore ..

Secretary ...

Sergeant at Arms ..

Chaplain ....

Secretary to the Majority ..

Secretary to the Minority ..

The Senate elects all its officers except its president, who is the Vice-President of the United States. If the Vice-President is absent or has become the President of the United States, the president pro tempore (or "pro tem") of the Senate serves in his place.

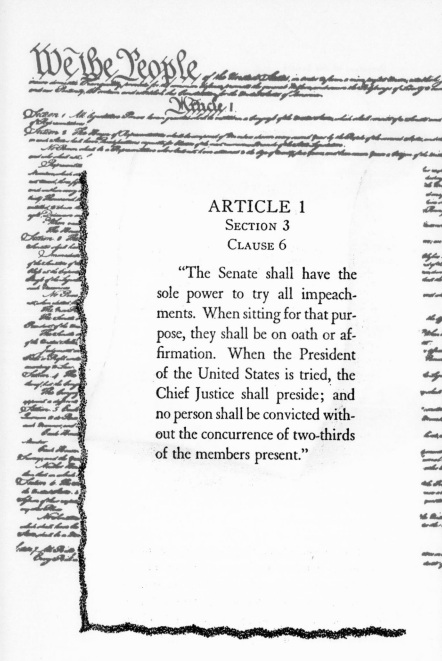

# ARTICLE 1
## SECTION 3
### CLAUSE 6

"The Senate shall have the sole power to try all impeachments. When sitting for that purpose, they shall be on oath or affirmation. When the President of the United States is tried, the Chief Justice shall preside; and no person shall be convicted without the concurrence of two-thirds of the members present."

President of the Senate

"And it is further charged . . ."

Senators

Defendant

When a government official is accused of a crime, the House of Representatives charges him with that crime by voting to impeach him (see page 26). The Senate alone is allowed to decide whether he is innocent or guilty. If the President of the United States is to be tried, the Chief Justice of the United States, not the

Chief Justice
of the Supreme Court

Senators

President
of the U.S.

Vice-President, presides over the Senate. The Constitution orders that the accused person shall be considered innocent unless two-thirds of the Senators present agree that he is guilty.

*You give:* To the Senate the right to remove government officials from office.

*You get:* Careful judgments from the Senate after the House has made its accusations.

# ARTICLE 1
## SECTION 3
## CLAUSE 7

"Judgment in cases of impeachment shall not extend further than to removal from office, and disqualification to hold and enjoy any office of honor, trust, or profit under the United States: but the party convicted shall nevertheless be liable and subject to indictment, trial, judgment, and punishment, according to law."

## JUDGMENT IN CASES OF IMPEACHMENT

In an impeachment trial, the official can be punished only by

a) Being removed from office.

b) Being forbidden to hold any office of honor, trust, or profit under the United States.

This clause gives rules for punishing an impeached official if he is found guilty. The Senate can punish him only by taking his position away and forbidding him ever to hold any other position in the federal government. If the Senate could punish him more severely, he would be losing his right to a jury trial (see pages 206–7).

After his trial by the Senate, the official may still be tried in a regular court and be given the usual punishments for his crimes.

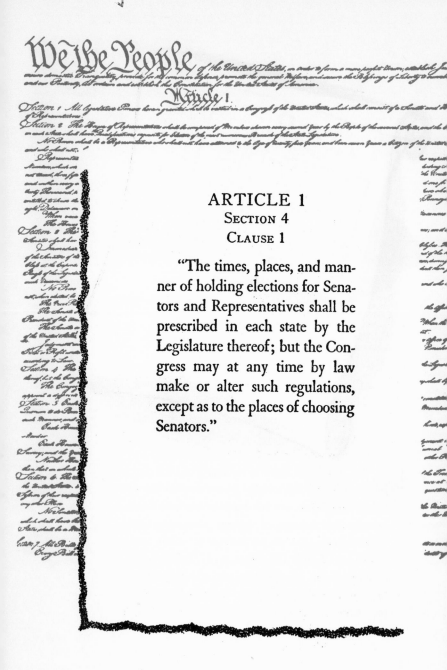

# ARTICLE 1
## SECTION 4
## CLAUSE 1

"The times, places, and manner of holding elections for Senators and Representatives shall be prescribed in each state by the Legislature thereof; but the Congress may at any time by law make or alter such regulations, except as to the places of choosing Senators."

Elections are held
in even-numbered years

All states except one hold Congressional elections on the Tuesday after the first Monday in November of even-numbered years (1952, 1954, and so on). Maine holds its elections in September.

The Constitution leaves nearly all election regulations to the states. However, it allows Congress to pass certain laws to safeguard the honesty and fairness of national elections. One law requires that secret ballots be used. Another law limits the amount of money that candidates for the Senate and the House of Representatives may spend during campaigns for election.

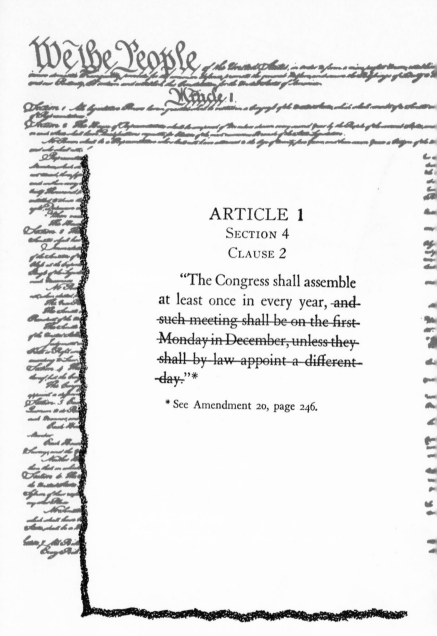

# ARTICLE 1
## SECTION 4
### CLAUSE 2

"The Congress shall assemble
at least once in every year, ~~and
such meeting shall be on the first
Monday in December, unless they
shall by law appoint a different
day.~~"*

* See Amendment 20, page 246.

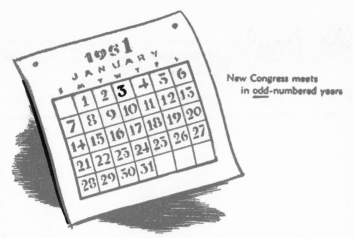

New Congress meets
in <u>odd</u>-numbered years

The kings of European countries sometimes kept their legislatures from holding regular meetings. This clause makes sure that Congress shall not be kept from meeting regularly and will not neglect its duties.

Amendment 20 (see page 246) orders that the new Congress shall meet on January 3 of each odd-numbered year following the regular November elections. This is called the first session of that particular Congress. Congress meets again for a second session on January 3 of each even-numbered year. Also, the President has power to call Congress into special session if necessary (see page 136). A session lasts as long as there is work to be done.

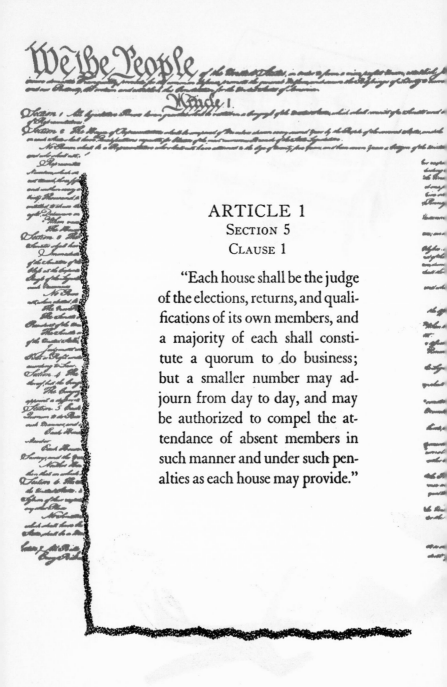

# ARTICLE 1
## SECTION 5
### CLAUSE 1

"Each house shall be the judge of the elections, returns, and qualifications of its own members, and a majority of each shall constitute a quorum to do business; but a smaller number may adjourn from day to day, and may be authorized to compel the attendance of absent members in such manner and under such penalties as each house may provide."

Returns and Qualifications

Sometimes persons have been elected to Congress in dishonest ways, or have failed to meet the requirements ordered by the Constitution. That is why Clause 1 gives each house of Congress the right to decide by a vote of the majority whether to keep any person from becoming a member of that house.

The same clause also says that each house can do business whenever it has a *quorum*—that is, when more than half its members are present. But, in practice, each house often carries on business even though fewer than half its members are present. This can be done provided that none of the members present objects to the lack of a quorum.

# ARTICLE 1
## Section 5
### Clause 2

"Each house may determine the rules of its proceedings, punish its members for disorderly behavior, and, with the concurrence of two-thirds, expel a member."

### Clause 3

"Each house shall keep a journal of its proceedings, and from time to time publish the same, excepting such parts as may in their judgment require secrecy; and the yeas and nays of the members of either house on any question shall, at the desire of one-fifth of those present, be entered on the journal."

### Clause 4

"Neither house, during the session of Congress, shall, without the consent of the other, adjourn for more than three days, nor to any other place than that in which the two houses shall be sitting."

Clause 3 directs Congress to keep a journal, or daily record, of its work. It does this by three official publications. The Senate has the *Senate Journal;* the House has the *House Journal.* Both are published at the end of each session of Congress. Congress as a whole has *The Congressional Record.* For many years it has been published every day that Congress has been in session. *The Congressional Record* helps Congressmen to keep track of their work and gives the people a chance to study the actions of their Congressmen.

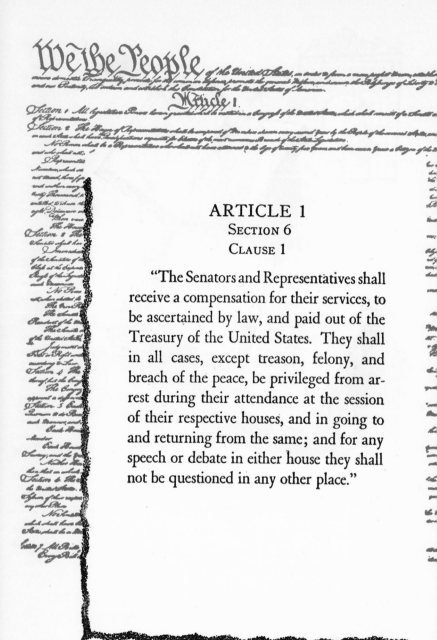

# ARTICLE 1
## SECTION 6
### CLAUSE 1

"The Senators and Representatives shall receive a compensation for their services, to be ascertained by law, and paid out of the Treasury of the United States. They shall in all cases, except treason, felony, and breach of the peace, be privileged from arrest during their attendance at the session of their respective houses, and in going to and returning from the same; and for any speech or debate in either house they shall not be questioned in any other place."

*You give:* To members of Congress (*a*) salaries, expenses, and other compensations; (*b*) freedom from arrest for ordinary reasons while doing their work; (*c*) freedom from arrest for anything they may say in Congress.

*You get:* A fearless expression of the thoughts of those in Congress. They might not risk speaking freely if they could be arrested or sued for what they say in Congress.

# ARTICLE 1
## SECTION 6
### CLAUSE 2

"No Senator or Representative shall, during the time for which he was elected, be appointed to any civil office under the authority of the United States, which shall have been created, or the emoluments whereof shall have been increased during such time; and no person holding any office under the United States shall be a member of either house during his continuance in office."

*You give:*  Orders that (*a*) no member of Congress, during his elected term, can take any United States government job which was either created or given a higher salary during his term in Congress; (*b*) anybody working in a United States government job must give up that job before becoming a member of Congress.

*You get:*  Protection from (*a*) members of Congress who might try to make highly paid government jobs for themselves; (*b*) too much power by Congress over the other branches of the government.

# ARTICLE 1
## Section 7
### Clause 1

"All bills for raising revenue shall originate in the House of Representatives; but the Senate may propose or concur with amendments as on other bills."

*You give:* To the House of Representatives the right to start all bills for raising money by taxes. The voters have more control over Representatives with two-year terms than they have over Senators with six-year terms.

*You get:* The opportunity every two years to vote your Representative out of office if he doesn't vote on tax bills as you think he should.

# ARTICLE 1
## SECTION 7
### CLAUSE 2

"Every bill which shall have passed the House of Representatives and the Senate, shall, before it becomes a law, be presented to the President of the United States; . . . ."

". . . . if he approve, he shall sign it, but if not, he shall return it, with his objections, to that house in which it shall have originated, . . . ."

"Veto" is a Latin word meaning "I forbid."

Most bills are passed if a majority in each house of Congress votes for them. The Constitution does not say this; but it names some exceptions, including vetoed bills, for which more than a majority vote is needed.

". . . . who shall enter the objections at large on their journal, and proceed to reconsider it."

"If after such reconsideration two-thirds of that house shall agree to pass the bill, it shall be sent, together with the objections, to the other house, by which it shall likewise be reconsidered, and if approved by two-thirds of that house, it shall become a law. But in all such cases the votes of both houses shall be determined by yeas and nays, and the names of the persons voting for and against the bill shall be entered on the journal of each house respectively."

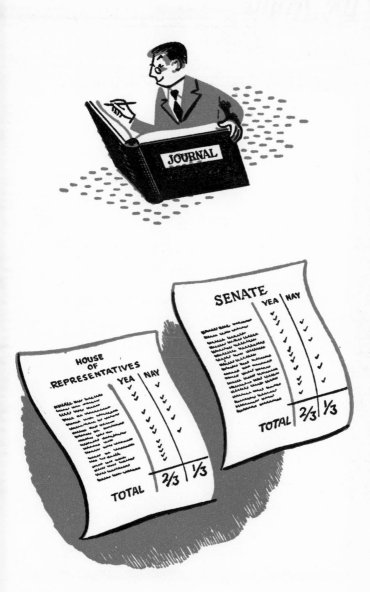

"If any bill shall not be returned by the President within ten days (Sundays excepted) after it shall have been presented to him, the same shall be a law, in like manner as if he had signed it, unless the Congress by their adjournment prevent its return, in which case it shall not be a law."

A bill becomes a law unless it is vetoed within <u>ten</u> days

*You give:* (*a*) To the President the right to approve or to veto all bills; (*b*) to Congress the task of persuading two-thirds of its members to vote for any bill that has been vetoed by the President, before that bill can become law.

*You get:* (*a*) Checks and balances between both houses of Congress and between Congress and the President; (*b*) protection against hasty and unwise actions either by Congress or by the President.

# ARTICLE 1
## SECTION 7
### CLAUSE 3

"Every order, resolution, or vote to which the concurrence of the Senate and House of Representatives may be necessary (except on a question of adjournment) shall be presented to the President of the United States; and before the same shall take effect, shall be approved by him, or being disapproved by him, shall be repassed by two-thirds of the Senate and the House of Representatives, according to the rules and limitations prescribed in the case of a bill."

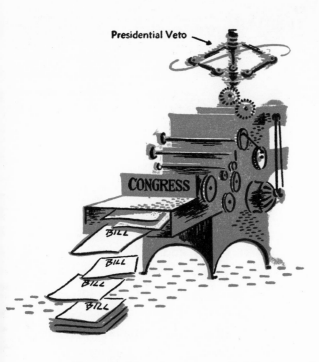

Presidential Veto

Some machines have parts called "governors" to keep them from going too fast. The presidential veto is the "governor" on the lawmaking machinery of the United States government. The veto helps to keep Congress from acting hastily.

*You give:* To the President the responsibility of signing or vetoing other kinds of measures, as well as bills, that have been passed by both houses of Congress.

*You get:* Another important check and balance in lawmaking.

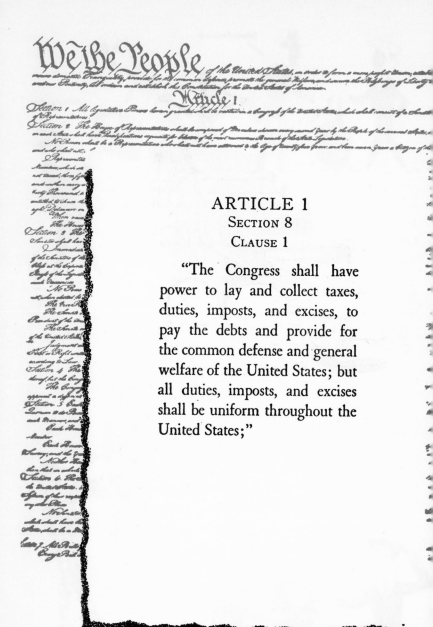

# ARTICLE 1
## SECTION 8
### CLAUSE 1

"The Congress shall have power to lay and collect taxes, duties, imposts, and excises, to pay the debts and provide for the common defense and general welfare of the United States; but all duties, imposts, and excises shall be uniform throughout the United States;"

This clause gives Congress the general power to collect taxes. Congress raises money by two kinds of taxes—direct taxes and indirect taxes. On page 23 you have read how Congress may impose direct taxes.

The indirect taxes which Congress may collect include taxes on goods from foreign countries. These are called duties or imposts. Another indirect tax is the excise tax. This is a tax on the manufacture and sale of many articles within the country, on certain business transactions, and so on. An indirect tax, unlike a direct tax, may be passed along from one person to another. A manufacturer pays the government a tax on an article, but includes that tax in the price he charges the wholesaler. The wholesaler includes that tax in the price he charges the retailer. Finally you, the consumer, pay the tax as part of the price of the article.

Congress may use its taxing powers to get money

"to pay the debts

"and provide for the common defense

"and general welfare of the United States

".... but all duties, imposts, and excises shall be uniform throughout the United States."

Indirect taxes must be the same throughout the country. A federal tax on automobiles, for example, or on theater tickets, tobacco, or cosmetics, shall be the same in San Francisco as in New York and New Orleans.

*You give:* Power to Congress to collect the money needed: (*a*) to protect the nation against foreign countries; (*b*) to take care of other needs within the country.

*You get:* (*a*) A federal government that is strong enough to carry out the duties given to it by the Constitution, and that can pay the costs of carrying out these duties; (*b*) a fair and uniform system of taxation.

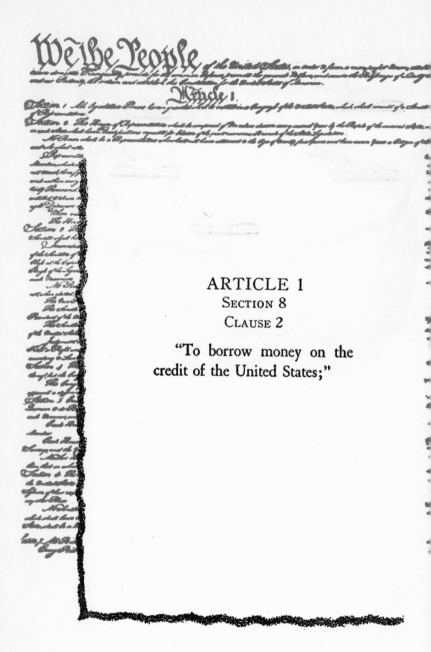

# ARTICLE 1
## SECTION 8
## CLAUSE 2

"To borrow money on the
credit of the United States;"

*You give:* (a) Power to Congress to borrow money needed to carry on the work of government; (b) part of your taxes to pay back the money, with interest, that the government borrows.

*You get:* (a) The services and protection of the government; (b) interest on money you lend to the government.

# ARTICLE 1
## SECTION 8
### CLAUSE 3

"To regulate commerce with foreign nations, . . . ."

". . . . and among the several states, and with the Indian tribes;"

The first part of this clause gives Congress complete power over trade between the United States and foreign countries. Using this authority, Congress has passed laws applying to (1) goods entering or leaving the country, (2) ships and other means of transportation and communication, and (3) foreign people who may come to the United States.

Under this broad power, all our laws which apply to foreign trade are made by the federal government. This keeps the states from getting us into trouble by having different laws of their own. Also, states with important seaports are kept from taxing the trade of other states.

*You give:* To Congress complete control over foreign commerce. This control includes the following powers: (*a*) to collect tariffs, or taxes, on imported goods; (*b*) to keep out harmful products; (*c*) to control immigration; (*d*) to keep goods needed here from being sent to other countries; (*e*) to help transportation and communication by land, sea, and air.

*You get:* (*a*) Money collected as tariff to help in running the government; (*b*) protection of American industries from unfair foreign competition; (*c*) safeguards for American health and morals; (*d*) protection from too many people, or from undesirable people, coming to the United States from foreign countries; (*e*) conservation of forests, water, soil, minerals, and other natural resources; (*f*) operation of lighthouses, dredging of harbors and rivers, and other aids to shipping; (*g*) uniform regulation of international trade.

The power to regulate interstate commerce is granted to Congress in the second part of Clause 3. Our government has found this power important in adapting itself to the growth of our country from a simple farming nation to a nation with many great industries.

The interstate commerce which Congress may regulate includes all the things that cross state boundaries—goods, persons, and words. This power to regulate also includes all the means by which these things move. These means are railroads, ships and the rivers on which they travel, trucks and busses, air lines, telegraph and telephone lines, and radio and television stations. It also includes things that are done wholly in one state but are, nevertheless, a step in interstate commerce, such as raising apples in Washington for shipment to markets in the Middle West.

Any state law or tax may be declared unconstitutional if it interferes with interstate commerce or with the regulation of that commerce by Congress. For example, Idaho could not tax apples being shipped through that state from Washington to Middle Western markets; Indiana could not have a law to keep out automobiles made in Michigan.

*You give:* To Congress authority: (*a*) to regulate interstate commerce; (*b*) to supervise trade with the Indians.

*You get:* (*a*) Free flow of goods among all the states; (*b*) encouragement and supervision of transportation and communication by land, sea, and air; (*c*) a check on the movement of harmful goods or persons; (*d*) protection of Indians from persons who might take advantage of them.

# ARTICLE 1
## Section 8
## Clause 4

"To establish a uniform rule of naturalization, . . . ."

".. . . and uniform laws on the subject of bankruptcies throughout the United States;"

*You give:* To Congress the power to decide which foreign-born persons may become citizens of the United States, and how they may do so.

*You get:* As new residents of the United States only those foreign-born persons who deserve to become citizens.

*You give:* To Congress the power to pass laws which protect both an individual who owes more money than he can pay and those to whom he owes it.

*You get:* A single set of laws for the whole country which (*a*) protect you from losing all that you own if you should fall into serious debt; and (*b*) guarantee you your fair share of the property of someone who owes debts to you and to other persons.

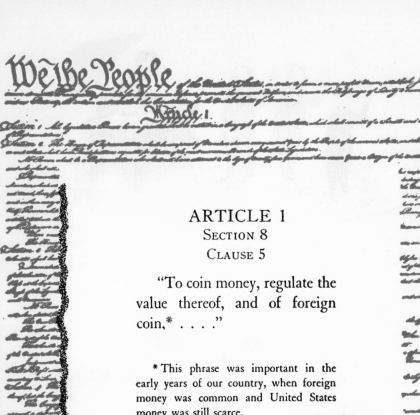

# ARTICLE 1
## SECTION 8
## CLAUSE 5

"To coin money, regulate the value thereof, and of foreign coin,* . . . ."

* This phrase was important in the early years of our country, when foreign money was common and United States money was still scarce.

". . . . and fix the standard of weights and measures;"

*You give:* To Congress permission to turn out money (both coins and bills) and to decide how much that money is worth.

*You get:* Money that has the same appearance and value throughout the country.

*You give:* To Congress the power to set up a single system of weights and measures.

*You get:* Uniform weights and measures. For example, in all of the states, one pound weighs sixteen ounces, one mile is exactly 5,280 feet, and a yard is 36 inches.

# ARTICLE 1
## Section 8
## Clause 6

"To provide for the punishment of counterfeiting the securities and current coin of the United States;"

## Clause 7

"To establish post offices and post roads;"

*You give:* Power to Congress to punish people who make or use counterfeit money or false government bonds.

*You get:* A government service which protects the value of your money and bonds.

*You give:* To Congress authority (*a*) to set up a postal system; (*b*) to help in developing the land, water, and air routes over which the mail is hauled.

*You get:* (*a*) Uniform postage rates; (*b*) national distribution of mail at low cost; (*c*) better systems of transportation and communication.

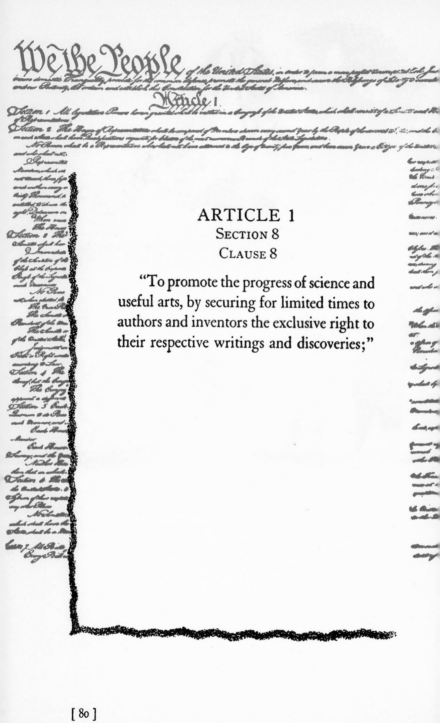

# ARTICLE 1
## SECTION 8
### CLAUSE 8

"To promote the progress of science and useful arts, by securing for limited times to authors and inventors the exclusive right to their respective writings and discoveries;"

*You give:* To Congress the power to pass laws that allow inventors, authors, and artists, for a limited number of years, to keep anyone else from making or selling their work without their permission.

*You get:* (*a*) A chance to use and enjoy the many things created by American inventors, authors, and artists; (*b*) the right to enjoy the money and fame that may come from anything you invent or create.

# ARTICLE 1
## Section 8
### Clause 9

"To constitute tribunals inferior to the Supreme Court;"

### Clause 10

"To define and punish piracies and felonies committed on the high seas, and offenses against the law of nations;"

***You give:*** Authority to Congress to set up federal courts which are lower than the Supreme Court. (For information about the Supreme Court, see page 145.)

***You get:*** A system of federal courts that can be changed as needed to fit the changes in the country and its people (see also page 148).

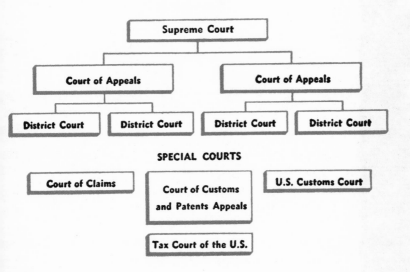

***You give:*** Power to Congress to maintain law and order outside the boundaries of the United States when United States citizens are concerned.

***You get:*** (*a*) Protection and control of citizens and ships of the United States when they are out of the country; (*b*) protection against quarrels between the United States and other nations resulting from wrong actions of United States citizens.

# ARTICLE 1
## SECTION 8
### CLAUSE 11

"To declare war, grant letters of marque and reprisal,* and make rules concerning captures on land and water;"

* This power was important when private citizens were permitted to capture enemy ships. It is no longer used.

When a nation goes to war, it is in danger. And so are the lives of its citizens. That is why the Constitution orders in this clause that only Congress—elected by the people—has the right to declare war. But a war may be started by a foreign country, as when Japan attacked Hawaii in 1941. Or, the President, as commander in chief of the armed forces, may decide to use these forces to protect the United States from foreign attack. Congress may then meet to declare "that a state of war exists."

*You give:* Power to Congress (*a*) to declare war; (*b*) to set up rules for capturing the property of enemy countries or of neutral countries which help the enemy.

*You get:* Assurance that after studying the facts, Congress, and only Congress, may declare war.

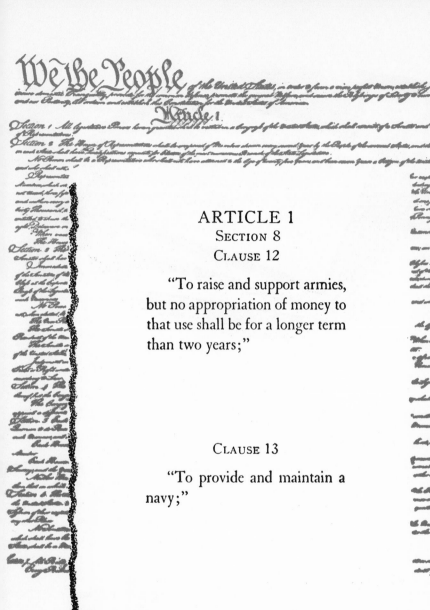

# ARTICLE 1
## SECTION 8
### CLAUSE 12

"To raise and support armies, but no appropriation of money to that use shall be for a longer term than two years;"

### CLAUSE 13

"To provide and maintain a navy;"

## FOR TWO YEARS ONLY

These clauses give Congress great military power. Congress can draft citizens into the armed forces and make them obey military law. It can buy all the articles the armed forces need. The makers of the Constitution wanted to be sure that Congress would never lose control of the armed forces. That was why they ordered that Congress should never grant the army more money than it would need for two years. Actually, Congress grants money to the armed forces every year.

*You give:* Power to Congress to raise armies and pay for them.

*You get:* Assurance (*a*) that the armies will be ready when needed; (*b*) that the armed forces will be controlled by Congress.

*You give:* To Congress power to set up and support the Navy.

*You get:* A navy that is always ready to protect the nation.

# ARTICLE 1
## Section 8
### Clause 14

"To make rules for the government and regulation of the land and naval forces;"

### Clause 15

"To provide for calling forth the militia to execute the laws of the Union, suppress insurrections, and repel invasions;"

### Clause 16

"To provide for organizing, arming, and disciplining the militia, and for governing such part of them as may be employed in the service of the United States, reserving to the states, respectively, the appointment of the officers, and the authority of training the militia according to the discipline prescribed by Congress;"

The organized militia, or armies of the states, are known as the National Guard. The federal government now pays most of the expenses for training and equipping them. It can take them into the United States Army in time of war, or can use them at other times to keep law and order.

*You give:* To Congress the power to keep the National Guard trained and equipped for emergencies.

*You get:* A group of citizens with military training who can be added to the regular Army if needed.

# ARTICLE 1
## Section 8
### Clause 17

"To exercise exclusive legislation in all cases whatsoever over such district (not exceeding ten miles square) as may, by cession of particular states and the acceptance of Congress, become the seat of government of the United States, and to exercise like authority over all places purchased by the consent of the Legislature of the state in which the same shall be, for the erection of forts, magazines, arsenals, dockyards, and other needful buildings;—And"

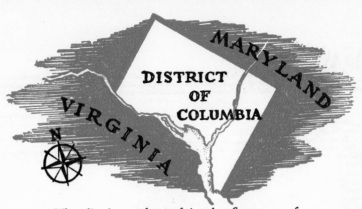

The district spoken of in the first part of this clause is the District of Columbia. In this district is the city of Washington, headquarters of the national government. The District of Columbia is governed by Congress. Its business is run by a board of three commissioners. They are chosen by the President with the consent of the Senate.

The United States government is the greatest property owner in the nation. It owns parks, forests, military posts, courthouses, post offices, and many other properties throughout the country.

*You give:* To Congress permission to buy and control whatever property the national government needs to carry out its duties.

*You get:* The use of parks, post offices, and many other properties and services owned and operated by your government.

# ARTICLE 1
## SECTION 8
## CLAUSE 18

"To make all laws which shall be necessary and proper for carrying into execution the foregoing powers, and all other powers vested by this Constitution in the government of the United States, or in any department or officer thereof."

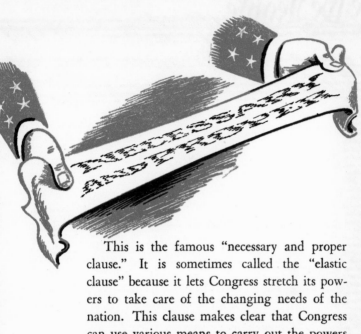

This is the famous "necessary and proper clause." It is sometimes called the "elastic clause" because it lets Congress stretch its powers to take care of the changing needs of the nation. This clause makes clear that Congress can use various means to carry out the powers given to it by the Constitution. For example, Congress has power to control foreign and interstate commerce. And, because of this clause, Congress also has the power to improve rivers and harbors to aid such commerce. The Supreme Court, of course, has the power to decide whether any action which Congress considers "necessary and proper" is constitutional.

*You give:* Power to Congress to make such laws as may be necessary and proper for the federal government to carry out its duties.

*You get:* Assurance that the government, even when faced by changing conditions, can always do its work as ordered by the Constitution.

# ARTICLE 1
## Section 9
### Clause 1

"~~The migration or importation of such persons as any of the states now existing shall think proper to admit, shall not be prohibited by the Congress prior to the year one thousand eight hundred and eight, but a tax or duty may be imposed on such importation, not exceeding ten dollars for each person.~~"*

* This clause referred to the slave trade. It was a restriction, until the year 1808, on the power of Congress to regulate foreign trade.

### Clause 2

"The privilege of the writ of habeas corpus shall not be suspended, unless when in cases of rebellion or invasion the public safety may require it."

Clause 2 orders that the people of the United States shall be protected by the right of *habeas corpus*.* By using his right of habeas corpus, a person who has been arrested can force the jailer to take him to a judge. If it can be proved that there is good reason for holding him, he must be charged with a crime. If not, he must be set free.

In some countries, kings and dictators have put people into prison without accusing them of a crime or giving them a trial. Habeas corpus keeps this from happening in the United States. The right of habeas corpus may be set aside only in times of war or rebellion. The right goes back into effect as soon as the danger is over.

* The words "habeas corpus" mean literally "you may have the body." They are the beginning of a Latin sentence which means that the prisoner must be brought before the court.

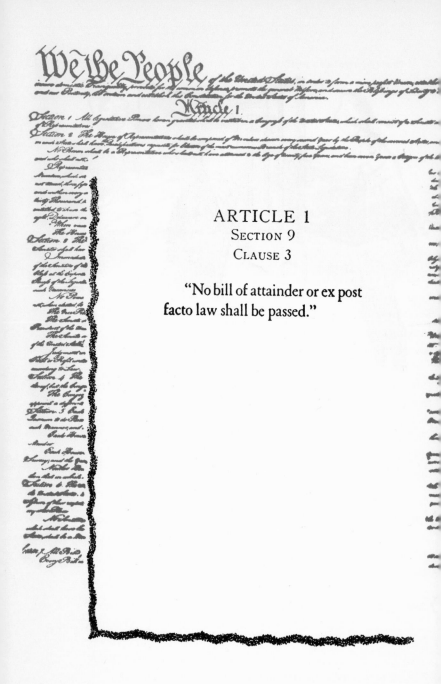

# ARTICLE 1
## SECTION 9
## CLAUSE 3

"No bill of attainder or ex post facto law shall be passed."

A bill of attainder is a law passed by a legislature to punish a person without letting him have a regular trial in court. It is another way in which an unjust government sometimes punishes a person who disagrees with it.

"Ex post facto" is a Latin phrase meaning "after the deed." An ex post facto law is one that punishes people for earlier actions of theirs that were not crimes before the law was passed. Under this clause, if a law is passed today, it may not be used to punish a person for something he did yesterday.

*You deny:* To Congress any right (*a*) to punish a person without a regular trial in court; (*b*) to declare any act a crime that was not a crime at the time the act was committed.

*You get:* Assurance (*a*) that no one will receive punishment because of a special act passed by Congress in order to punish only him; (*b*) that if you know what the law is and obey it, you will not be convicted of a crime.

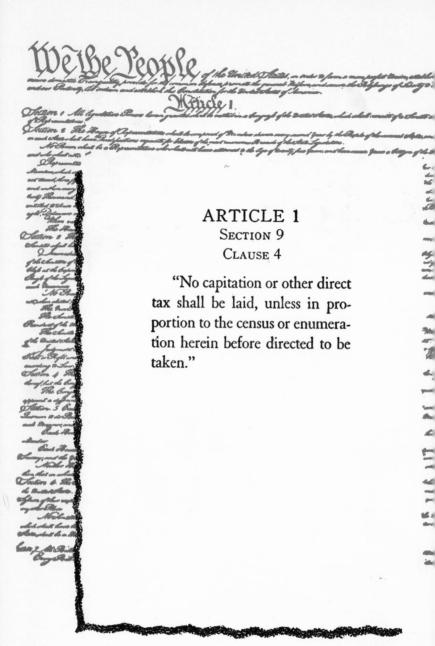

# ARTICLE 1
## Section 9
### Clause 4

"No capitation or other direct tax shall be laid, unless in proportion to the census or enumeration herein before directed to be taken."

An earlier clause in Article 1 says that direct taxes must be divided among the states according to their populations (see page 21). The meaning of that clause is made clearer by Clause 4 of Section 9. Clause 4 says that Congress can levy a direct tax only in proportion to the numbers of people within the different states.

A capitation tax is a direct tax which collects money from every person. This clause directs that any national capitation tax must be the same for persons in every state. Some other direct taxes are those on lands or buildings.

Congress has seldom ordered direct taxes. One of them is the federal income tax, which in some ways is like an indirect tax. In 1913, Amendment 16 was added to the Constitution. This amendment gave Congress the right to tax incomes (see page 239).

# ARTICLE 1
## Section 9
### Clause 5

"No tax or duty shall be laid on articles exported from any state."

### Clause 6

"No preference shall be given by any regulation of commerce or revenue to the ports of one state over those of another; nor shall vessels bound to, or from, one state be obliged to enter, clear, or pay duties to another."

This clause keeps Congress from penalizing any state by taxing the goods sent out of that state. It also encourages our manufacturers and farmers to trade with other countries.

**You deny:** To Congress any power to tax goods being shipped out of the country.

**You get:** Benefits of world trade.

Under the Constitution the states gave up their powers to control trade with other states or countries. But the rules in Clause 6 were written to keep Congress from misusing the powers that the states had given up. This clause means that Congress must not pass laws to help the trade of one state or hurt the trade of another state, but must treat all states alike. Ships must be allowed to go freely from state to state.

**You deny:** To Congress any right to give the shipping of one state an advantage over the shipping of another state.

**You get:** Equal opportunity for the commerce of all parts of the country.

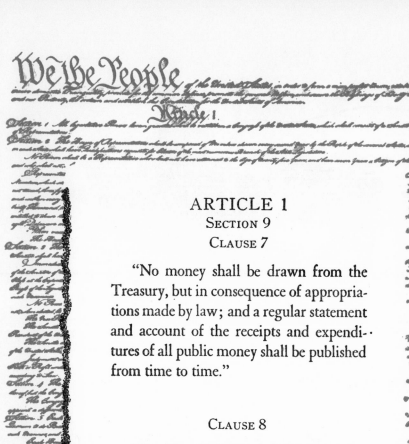

# ARTICLE 1
## Section 9
### Clause 7

"No money shall be drawn from the Treasury, but in consequence of appropriations made by law; and a regular statement and account of the receipts and expenditures of all public money shall be published from time to time."

### Clause 8

"No title of nobility shall be granted by the United States; and no person holding any office of profit or trust under them shall, without the consent of the Congress, accept of any present, emolument, office, or title, of any kind whatever, from any king, prince, or foreign state."

*You deny:* The right of anybody in the government to spend money from the United States Treasury unless a law says that such spending is a proper use of public money.

*You get:* (*a*) Assurance that public money is spent only for a lawful purpose; (*b*) an opportunity to see how public money is being spent.

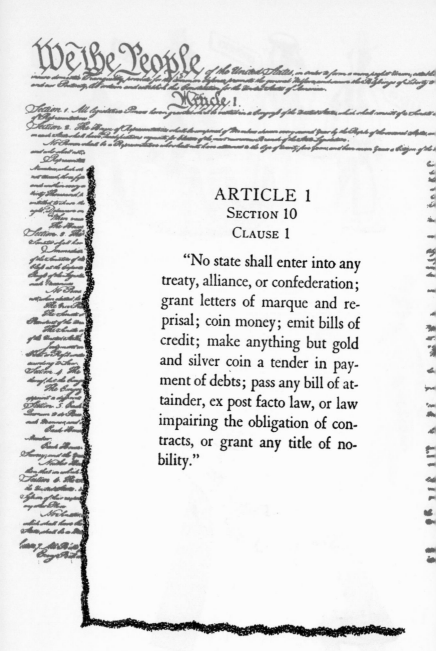

# ARTICLE 1
## Section 10
### Clause 1

"No state shall enter into any treaty, alliance, or confederation; grant letters of marque and reprisal; coin money; emit bills of credit; make anything but gold and silver coin a tender in payment of debts; pass any bill of attainder, ex post facto law, or law impairing the obligation of contracts, or grant any title of nobility."

"You states must all keep an eye on this clause! It forbids you to do certain things which the federal government can do better. And it forbids you to do certain things which the people don't intend to have anybody do!"

*You deny:* To the states the rights (*a*) to make treaties, coin money, or use other powers which the Constitution gives to the federal government; or (*b*) to do certain other things, including the punishment of a person without a trial in court.

*You get:* Assurances (*a*) that no state will take over certain duties assigned to the federal government; (*b*) that no state will take certain powers which you do not intend to give to anyone.

# ARTICLE 1
## SECTION 10
### CLAUSE 2

"No state shall, without the consent of the Congress, lay any imposts or duties on imports or exports, except what may be absolutely necessary for executing its inspection laws; and the net produce of all duties and imposts, laid by any state on imports or exports, shall be for the use of the Treasury of the United States; and all such laws shall be subject to the revision and control of the Congress."

This clause keeps states with busy harbors from making the people of other states pay taxes for the right to use those harbors for foreign commerce. But states may charge inspection fees, such as those for inspecting foods or other products shipped in from other states.

*You deny:* To the state any right to tax goods moving across its borders except as needed to pay normal costs of inspection.

*You get:* A flow of commerce that is taxed only by the federal government. These taxes are the same for every state.

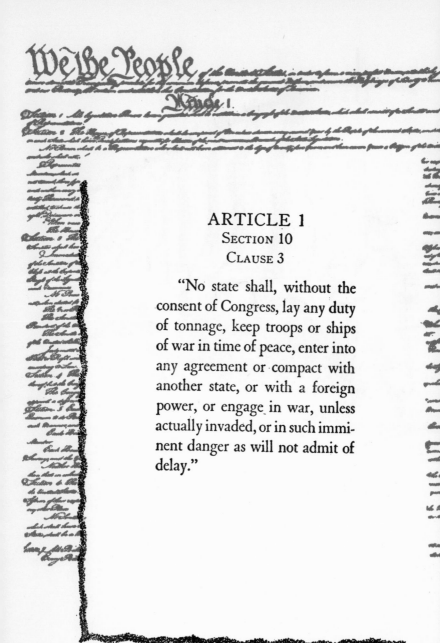

# ARTICLE 1
## SECTION 10
### CLAUSE 3

"No state shall, without the consent of Congress, lay any duty of tonnage, keep troops or ships of war in time of peace, enter into any agreement or compact with another state, or with a foreign power, or engage in war, unless actually invaded, or in such imminent danger as will not admit of delay."

"Duty of tonnage" is a tax that must be paid as a ship enters a port. The size of the tax depends on the number of tons of cargo the ship is carrying. The states may not collect such a tax unless Congress says they may.

Agreements, or compacts, between states, made with the permission of Congress, are not uncommon. For example, New York and New Jersey agreed to set up the Port of New York Authority. This authority built the George Washington Bridge over the Hudson River and dug tunnels under it. Such agreements are useful in handling problems between states.

# ARTICLE

## 2

The White House

## THE EXECUTIVE BRANCH
## CARRIES OUT THE LAWS

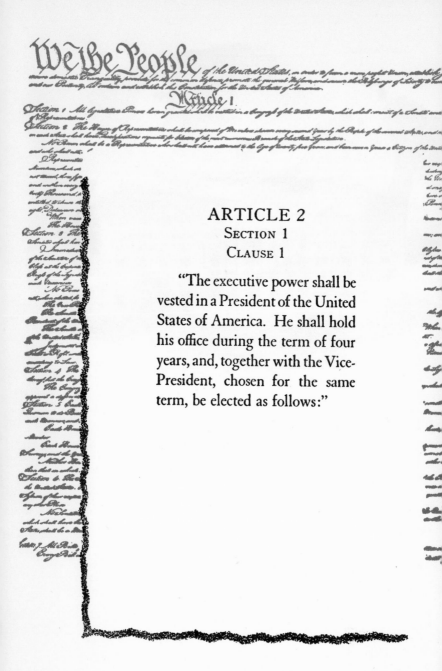

# ARTICLE 2
## SECTION 1
### CLAUSE 1

"The executive power shall be vested in a President of the United States of America. He shall hold his office during the term of four years, and, together with the Vice-President, chosen for the same term, be elected as follows:"

Vice-President                    President

Article 2 sets up the second great branch of our government. It is the executive branch, which carries out, or executes, the laws passed by Congress. The Constitution gives this executive power and responsibility to the President. Thousands of people help him, but his job is still one of the hardest and most important in the world. The Constitution also provides for a Vice-President. He can step into the President's job at a moment's notice if the President should die or if he should be unable to carry on his duties.

*You give:* Full power to the President of the United States to carry out all the executive duties of the country.

*You get:* An officer of the government who is in a position of great power and can therefore make sure that the nation's laws are carried out.

# ARTICLE 2
## SECTION 1
### CLAUSE 2

"Each state shall appoint, in such manner as the Legislature thereof may direct, a number of electors, equal to the whole number of Senators and Representatives to which the state may be entitled in the Congress: but no Senator or Representative, or person holding an office of trust or profit under the United States, shall be appointed an elector."

### CLAUSE 3

"The electors shall meet in their respective states and vote by ballot for two persons, of whom one at least shall not be an inhabitant of the same state with themselves. And they shall make a list of all the persons voted for, and of the number of votes for each, which list they shall sign and certify and transmit, sealed, to the seat of the government of the United States, directed to the president of the Senate. The president of the Senate shall, in the pres-

The makers of the Constitution felt that the President and the Vice-President could best be chosen by a small group of men specially selected for this purpose. They planned, therefore, that the state legislatures should choose a special group of electors to vote for these two important offices. These electors make up what

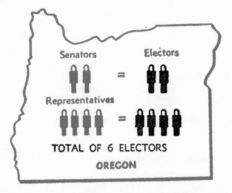

is called the "Electoral College," but they never meet as a single group. Instead they meet at their state capitols. Here they cast their votes and then report the results to the president of the Senate.

According to the original plan in the Constitution, the votes from the Electoral College were to be counted in Congress and the person with the most votes was to be President. The person with the next most votes was to be Vice-President. But changes were soon made in this plan. Amendment 12, adopted in 1804, ruled that the electors must show which man they wanted for President and which for Vice-President.

Early in the 1800's, our present system of

ence of the Senate and the House of Representatives, open all the certificates, and the votes shall then be counted. The person having the greatest number of votes shall be the President, if such number be a majority of the whole number of electors appointed; and if there be more than one who have such majority, and have an equal number of votes, then the House of Representatives shall immediately choose by ballot one of them for President; and if no person have a majority, then from the five highest on the list the said House shall in like manner choose the President. But in choosing the President, the vote shall be taken by states, the representation from each state having one vote. A quorum for this purpose shall consist of a member or members from two-thirds of the states, and a majority of all the states shall be necessary to a choice. In every case, after the choice of the President, the person having the greatest number of votes of the electors shall be the Vice President. But if there should remain two or more who have equal votes, the Senate shall choose from them by ballot the Vice President."*

* Changed by Amendment 12 (page 222).

political parties began. This system brought about a still more important change in the presidential elections. The change was never put into the Constitution, but came about as a result of custom.

The writers of the Constitution intended that the Electoral College should give careful thought to choosing the best man in the country as President. But when the political parties became powerful, the leaders of each party in Congress decided who should be that party's candidate for President. Each party then got various groups of electors to promise to vote for its candidate.

After 1830, political leaders from all parts of the country began meeting every four years in national party conventions. At its convention each party chose men to be its candidates for President and Vice-President. It also decided on the party's *platform*—that is, a statement of what its candidates would do if they were elected.

That was how our present customs for presidential elections began. On the ballot, you actually vote for the electors belonging to your party; you do not vote for the candidates themselves. But this makes no real difference, since an elector never breaks his promise to vote for his party's candidates.

# ARTICLE 2
## Section 1
### Clause 4

"The Congress may determine the time of choosing the electors and the day on which they shall give their votes, which day shall be the same throughout the United States."

### Clause 5

"No person except a natural-born citizen, ~~or a citizen of the United States at the time of the adoption of this Constitution,~~ shall be eligible to the office of President; neither shall any person be eligible to that office who shall not have attained to the age of thirty-five years and been fourteen years a resident within the United States."

## THE PRESIDENT MUST BE:

1. A natural-born citizen of the United States.
2. Not less than thirty-five years of age.
3. A resident of the United States for at least fourteen years.

# ARTICLE 2
## SECTION 1
### CLAUSE 6

"In case of the removal of the President
from office, or of his death, resignation, or
inability to discharge the powers and duties
of the said office, the same shall devolve on
the Vice-President, and the Congress may
by law provide for the case of removal,
death, resignation, or inability, both of the
President and Vice-President, declaring
what officer shall then act as President, and
such officer shall act accordingly until the
disability be removed or a President shall
be elected."

President Franklin D. Roosevelt died in 1945 during World War II, and was succeeded by Vice-President Harry S. Truman. People then began worrying about what might happen if both the President and the Vice-President should die. In 1886 Congress had passed a law which said that if they both died the presidency should go to the Secretary of State and then to the other members of the President's Cabinet in a certain order. This would have meant that the presidency would go to a person appointed by the President, not to a person elected by the voters. In 1947, therefore, Congress changed the Law of Presidential Succession to read that the Vice-President should be followed by the Speaker of the House of Representatives and then by the president pro tempore of the Senate (see page 36). Both of these are elected officers of the government. If all four elected officers should die, which is not likely, then the Cabinet officers would be in line for the presidency.

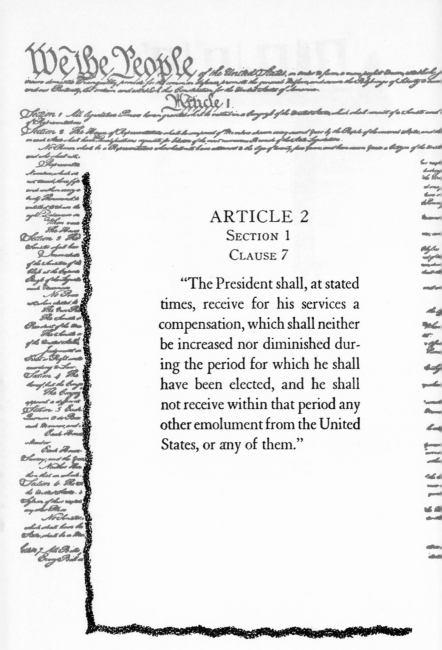

## ARTICLE 2
### Section 1
### Clause 7

"The President shall, at stated times, receive for his services a compensation, which shall neither be increased nor diminished during the period for which he shall have been elected, and he shall not receive within that period any other emolument from the United States, or any of them."

*You give:* Salary and expenses to the President. (You also give them to the Vice-President, although the Constitution does not mention payment to him.)

*You get:* A President who is free to do what he thinks is right; neither Congress nor anybody else can try to control him by changing his salary during his term.

## ARTICLE 2
### SECTION 1
### CLAUSE 8

"Before he enter on the execution of his office he shall take the following oath or affirmation: 'I do solemnly swear (or affirm) that I will faithfully execute the office of President of the United States, and will to the best of my ability, preserve, protect, and defend the Constitution of the United States.'"

A new President really becomes the **Presi-**
dent at the moment he takes the oath of office.
By custom the oath is given on Inauguration
Day by the Chief Justice of the United States,
in Washington, D.C.

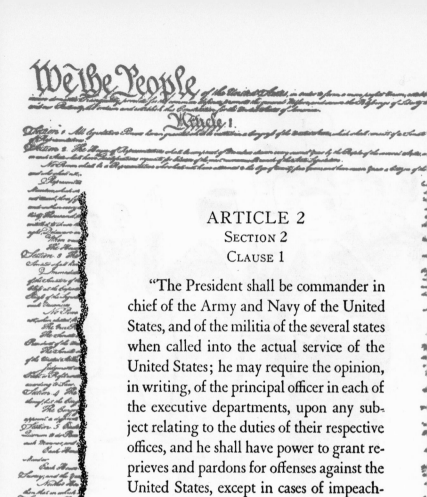

## ARTICLE 2
### Section 2
### Clause 1

"The President shall be commander in chief of the Army and Navy of the United States, and of the militia of the several states when called into the actual service of the United States; he may require the opinion, in writing, of the principal officer in each of the executive departments, upon any subject relating to the duties of their respective offices, and he shall have power to grant reprieves and pardons for offenses against the United States, except in cases of impeachment."

The office of the President of the United States is one of the most powerful positions in the world. There are only 320 words in the Constitution about the President's duties and powers (not counting what it says about his veto power). But those few words, in Sections 2 and 3 of Article 2, give him powers of many kinds.

**Commander in Chief**
OF
**The Armed Forces**
AND OF
**The Militia**
OF THE SEVERAL STATES
WHEN IN SERVICE OF
THE UNITED STATES

When the makers of the Constitution made the President commander in chief of the armed forces, they were thinking of several important points: (1) They ordered that the head of the armed forces should be elected by the people. (2) They prevented any military officer of the armed forces from seizing the government and making himself President. (3) They also prevented any President from becoming a dictator, since he can be head of the armed forces only as long as he is President—and a President can be impeached (see page 39) or voted out of office. (4) They placed in the hands of one man the great governmental and military powers that must be used together in time of war.

"MAY GRANT REPRIEVES OR PARDONS FOR OFFENSES AGAINST THE UNITED STATES EXCEPT IN CASES OF IMPEACHMENT"

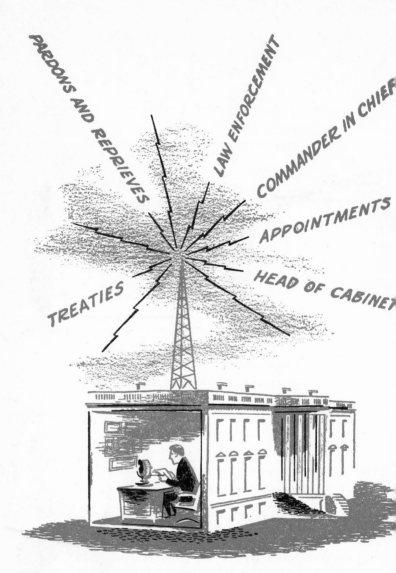

PARDONS AND REPRIEVES

LAW ENFORCEMENT

COMMANDER IN CHIEF

APPOINTMENTS

HEAD OF CABINET

TREATIES

**EXECUTIVE POWERS OF THE PRESIDENT**

In Clause 1, the words "principal officer in each of the executive departments" suggest that there will be various departments to help the President carry out his duties. The heads of these departments have come to be known as the President's Cabinet.

*You give:* Power to the President (*a*) to be head of all military forces; (*b*) to get advice from his Cabinet; (*c*) to pardon crimes against the United States when he thinks it wise.

*You get:* (*a*) Control of the armed forces by a civilian instead of a military person; (*b*) executive departments run by persons appointed by the President; (*c*) a "last chance" for anyone convicted of a crime against the national government.

# ARTICLE 2
## SECTION 2
### CLAUSE 2

"He shall have power, by and with the advice and consent of the Senate, to make treaties, provided two-thirds of the Senators present concur; and he shall nominate and, by and with the advice and consent of the Senate, shall appoint ambassadors, other public ministers and consuls, judges of the Supreme Court, and all other officers of the United States, whose appointments are not herein provided for, and which shall be established by law; but the Congress may by law vest the appointment of such inferior officers, as they think proper, in the President alone, in the courts of law, or in the heads of departments."

### CLAUSE 3

"The President shall have power to fill up all vacancies that may happen during the recess of the Senate, by granting commissions which shall expire at the end of their next session."

A treaty is an agreement between two or more countries. Usually our State Department works out and writes the agreement. After the President has approved the treaty, he must send it to the Senate. There, at least two-thirds of the Senators must agree to the treaty before it becomes law. This rule, that the Senate must approve of any treaty, keeps the President from making important agreements with other nations against the wishes of the elected representatives of the American people. But there are other kinds of foreign agreements, less important than treaties, which the President can make without the Senate's approval.

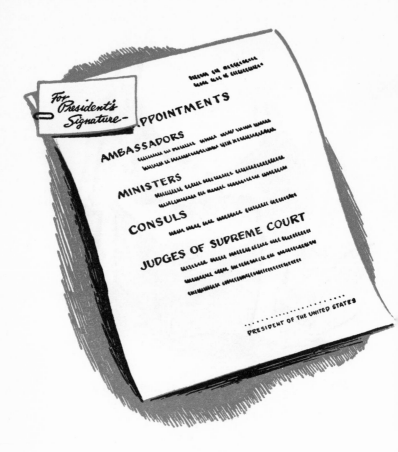

In Clause 2, the Constitution makes separate rules for selecting two different kinds of officers: (1) very important officers who are appointed by the President only after a majority of the Senate has approved them; and (2) inferior officers, who can be chosen by the President, by his Cabinet officers, or by judges without asking the Senate to approve them. These so-called "inferior officers" are not necessarily unimportant.

Among the very important officials whom the President can appoint only with the approval of the Senate are high officers of the armed forces, leading postmasters, head customs officials, and members of key agencies such as the Atomic Energy Commission, the Federal Reserve Board, and the Interstate Commerce Commission.

If one of these important jobs becomes vacant while Congress is not meeting, the President may choose a person for the job without waiting to get the Senate's permission. Such an appointment is known as an ad interim, or "for the interval," appointment. When Congress meets again, the Senate votes either for or against the person chosen by the President.

Only a few of the many people who work for the government ever see or talk with the President, the Cabinet officers, federal judges, or Senators. Most government workers get their jobs through the Civil Service Commission. The Commission finds the right people for the right jobs. The Commission gives examinations to people all over the country, for all kinds of jobs —from stenographers and laboratory technicians to forest rangers and airplane pilots. When there are job openings, they are offered to the people who made the highest scores in the civil service examinations. Thus, the government tries to find and keep the best person for a job, no matter what political party he belongs to.

Government employees have not always been selected so carefully. In earlier times, the people who had helped to elect the President were paid for their help by being given government jobs. To make jobs for these people, large numbers of government employees had to be fired. This was called the "Spoils System," from an old sentence which says: "To the victors belong the spoils"—that is, the rewards of victory belong to the people in the winning political party. The Spoils System did not bring the best workers into the government. Besides, it was unfair to the workers who were fired. But the Civil Service Commission we have today helps to keep the Spoils System out of government jobs.

*You give:* Power to the President (*a*) to make treaties with other countries if two-thirds of the Senate agrees to them; (*b*) to appoint many officials of the government, some with and some without consent of the Senate.

*You get:* (*a*) Thoughtful work by both the President and the Senate, so that this country can get along well with foreign countries; (*b*) careful choice of persons to fill important government offices.

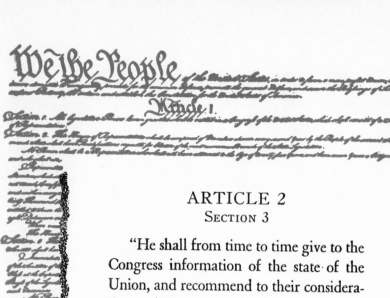

## ARTICLE 2
### SECTION 3

"He shall from time to time give to the Congress information of the state of the Union, and recommend to their consideration such measures as he shall judge necessary and expedient; he may, on extraordinary occasions, convene both houses, or either of them, and in case of disagreement between them, with respect to the time of adjournment, he may adjourn them to such time as he shall think proper; he shall receive ambassadors and other public ministers; he shall take care that the laws be faithfully executed, and shall commission all the officers of the United States."

# THE DUTIES OF THE PRESIDENT

The President of the United States is required
by the Constitution to carry out certain duties.

## DUTY 1—"STATE OF THE UNION" MESSAGE

**DUTY 2—HE SHALL RECEIVE AMBASSADORS
AND MINISTERS**

**DUTY 3—HE SHALL SEE THAT ALL LAWS
ARE EXECUTED**

**DUTY 4—HE SHALL COMMISSION ALL OFFICERS
OF THE UNITED STATES**

One of the President's duties is to give information and advice to Congress in messages on the "state of the Union." Hundreds of thousands of government employees throughout the country and around the world report back to their head officers. These officers in turn report to the President. Such messages are strong political tools for the President. Another tool is his power to call special sessions of Congress.

Among the most important duties of the President is "to take care that the laws be faithfully executed." He is too busy to do all this himself, but there are many officers in the executive branch of the government to help him enforce the laws.

*You give:* To the President (*a*) the duty of advising Congress about the nation's affairs; (*b*) the right to call special sessions of Congress; (*c*) the right to receive, or not to receive, the important officials sent to this country by foreign governments; (*d*) the responsibility for making sure that the nation's laws are enforced; (*e*) the duty of signing all documents appointing officials to office.

*You get:* (*a*) Expert reports on national affairs from time to time; (*b*) the certainty that Congress will be on the job when needed; (*c*) assurance that the laws passed by Congress will be enforced; (*d*) a final study by the President of all important appointments.

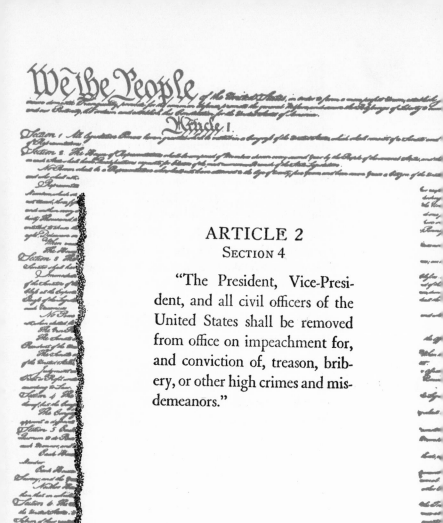

## ARTICLE 2
### SECTION 4

"The President, Vice-President, and all civil officers of the United States shall be removed from office on impeachment for, and conviction of, treason, bribery, or other high crimes and misdemeanors."

This section of the Constitution names some of the wrong acts for which the President and other government officials may be impeached (see pages 26, 27, and 39). If these officials are found guilty, they must be removed from their jobs.

It is treason for a citizen of the United States to make war against this country or to help the country's enemies. It is bribery to offer or accept money in return for special favors from the government. The "other high crimes and misdemeanors" are acts which are morally wrong or have been forbidden by laws.

# ARTICLE
# 3

The Supreme Court

## THE JUDICIAL BRANCH
## INTERPRETS THE LAWS

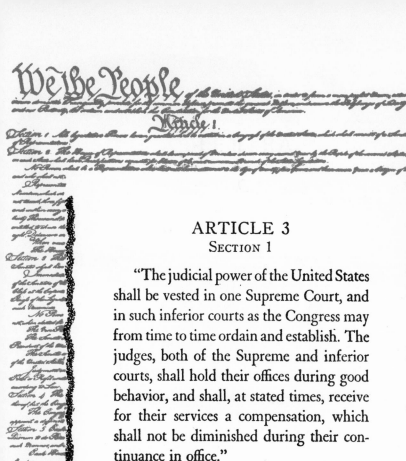

## ARTICLE 3
### SECTION 1

"The judicial power of the United States shall be vested in one Supreme Court, and in such inferior courts as the Congress may from time to time ordain and establish. The judges, both of the Supreme and inferior courts, shall hold their offices during good behavior, and shall, at stated times, receive for their services a compensation, which shall not be diminished during their continuance in office."

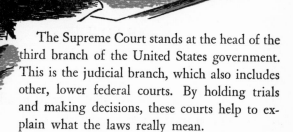

The Supreme Court stands at the head of the third branch of the United States government. This is the judicial branch, which also includes other, lower federal courts. By holding trials and making decisions, these courts help to explain what the laws really mean.

The judicial branch, and especially the Supreme Court, has the power to decide whether a federal, state, or local law is constitutional—that is, whether a law is permitted or forbidden by the Constitution. The Constitution does not say plainly that the Supreme Court shall have this great power, yet it has been used by the Court for more than a hundred years. The Supreme Court protects us from the other branches of our government by keeping them from getting too much power over us.

The "inferior courts" authorized by Congress are shown on page 83.

*You give:* (a) Authority to a system of federal courts to judge whether or not a law has been broken; (b) lasting jobs at good salaries to federal judges.

*You get:* (a) The same treatment under federal law in all states; (b) protection against unconstitutional laws; (c) experienced federal judges in a judicial branch independent of Congress, the President, the voters, or any political party.

# ARTICLE 3
## Section 2
### Clause 1

"The judicial power shall extend to all cases, in law and equity, arising under this Constitution, the laws of the United States, and treaties made, or which shall be made, under their authority; to all cases affecting ambassadors, other public ministers and consuls; to all cases of admiralty and maritime jurisdiction; to controversies to which the United States shall be a party; to controversies between two or more states, ~~between a state and citizens of another state,~~ between citizens of different states; between citizens of the same state claiming lands under grants of different states, and between a state, or the citizens thereof, and foreign states, citizens, or subjects."*

* The Eleventh Amendment, adopted in 1798, changed this clause slightly. When a citizen of another state or of a foreign nation wishes to sue a state, he must sue in the courts of that state under its own laws and with its consent.

Clause 1 of Section 2 names the kinds of cases which may be tried in federal courts. Most of these cases may be put into two general classes, as shown below:

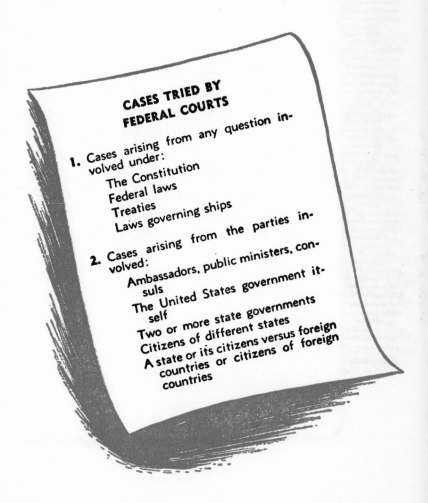

**CASES TRIED BY FEDERAL COURTS**

1. Cases arising from any question involved under:
   The Constitution
   Federal laws
   Treaties
   Laws governing ships

2. Cases arising from the parties involved:
   Ambassadors, public ministers, consuls
   The United States government itself
   Two or more state governments
   Citizens of different states
   A state or its citizens versus foreign countries or citizens of foreign countries

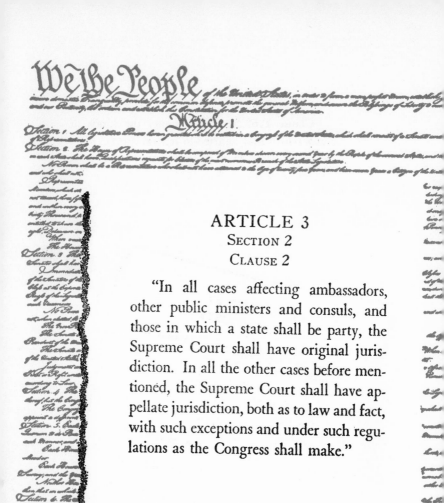

# ARTICLE 3
## Section 2
## Clause 2

"In all cases affecting ambassadors, other public ministers and consuls, and those in which a state shall be party, the Supreme Court shall have original jurisdiction. In all the other cases before mentioned, the Supreme Court shall have appellate jurisdiction, both as to law and fact, with such exceptions and under such regulations as the Congress shall make."

Certain cases, such as those concerning states or official representatives of foreign nations, are not tried in the lower federal courts. Instead they go at once to the Supreme Court. This is called the "original jurisdiction" of the Supreme Court.

Most other federal cases begin and end in the district courts, of which there is at least one in each state. But the Supreme Court has the right to look over the records of all such cases and to change the decisions of the lower courts if they are wrong. A case that has been tried in a local court, state court, or lower federal court may also be taken to the Supreme Court. This is called an "appeal of the case." The right of the Supreme Court to review decisions of other courts is called its "appellate jurisdiction." But so many cases are appealed that the Supreme Court cannot possibly review them all. Many of these cases are handled by the United States Courts of Appeal.

# ARTICLE 3
## SECTION 2
### CLAUSE 3

"The trial of all crimes, except in cases of impeachment, shall be by jury; and such trial shall be held in the state where the said crimes shall have been committed; but when not committed within any state, the trial shall be at such place or places as the Congress may by law have directed."*

* The provisions of this clause were expanded by Amendments 5, 6, and 7 (pages 204–9).

The word "crimes," as used in this part of the Constitution, does not include certain minor offenses. But it does include all other criminal offenses. These must be tried before a jury of citizens. This is a very important protection for every citizen.

*You give:* Orders (*a*) that when you are accused of a crime, your guilt or innocence must be decided by a jury; (*b*) that you must be tried in the state where your crime is said to have been committed.

*You get:* Protection from courts and judges who might imprison or fine you unjustly. The jury must decide the facts. All the jurors must agree that you are guilty before you can be punished.

# ARTICLE 3
## SECTION 3
### CLAUSE 1

"Treason against the United States shall consist only in levying war against them, or in adhering to their enemies, giving them aid and comfort. No person shall be convicted of treason unless on the testimony of two witnesses to the same overt act, or on confession in open court."

In earlier times, some people in England who had displeased the king were convicted of treason and sometimes were executed. To prevent the United States government from treating its own citizens so unjustly, the Constitution says what it means by "treason" and how a person may be convicted of it.

*You give:* (*a*) A definition of treason; (*b*) orders protecting you from punishment for treason unless you confess in open court or unless there are at least two witnesses against you.

*You get:* Protection (*a*) for your government against a very serious crime; (*b*) for yourself against **vague** or **false** charges of treason.

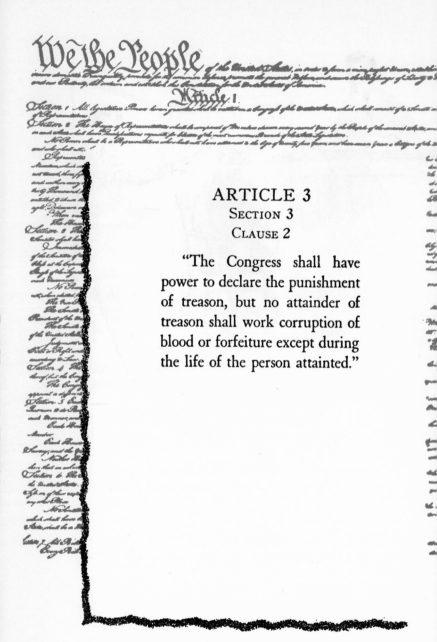

## ARTICLE 3
### SECTION 3
### CLAUSE 2

"The Congress shall have power to declare the punishment of treason, but no attainder of treason shall work corruption of blood or forfeiture except during the life of the person attainted."

The punishment ordered by Congress for treason is death, or not less than five years in prison and a $10,000 fine.

English rulers had sometimes punished the children of traitors by taking away their rights and their property. The second part of this clause of the Constitution protects the innocent relatives of a convicted traitor from unjust treatment.

*You give:* To Congress the power to set the punishment for treason, but you do not allow the traitor's relatives to be punished.

*You get:* (*a*) A certainty of severe punishment for one of the worst crimes that anyone can commit; (*b*) protection for innocent people.

# ARTICLE

# 4

## THE STATES AND THE
## FEDERAL GOVERNMENT

## ARTICLE 4
### SECTION 1

"Full faith and credit shall be given in each state to the public acts, records, and judicial proceedings of every other state. And the Congress may by general laws prescribe the manner in which such acts, records, and proceedings shall be proved, and the effect thereof."

There would be no end to mix-ups in the United States if the public acts—that is, the laws, the birth and death certificates, and the court decisions—of one state were not honored in the other states. This clause provides that these public acts within one state must be considered good in all the other states. Thus, if a court in your state orders your neighbor to pay you some money, your neighbor cannot get out of paying you by moving to another state. A court in another state will respect your right to the money as though that court itself had ordered the payment.

*You give:* Directions that each state shall respect the legal actions of every other state.

*You get:* Respect in every state for your legal rights in your own state.

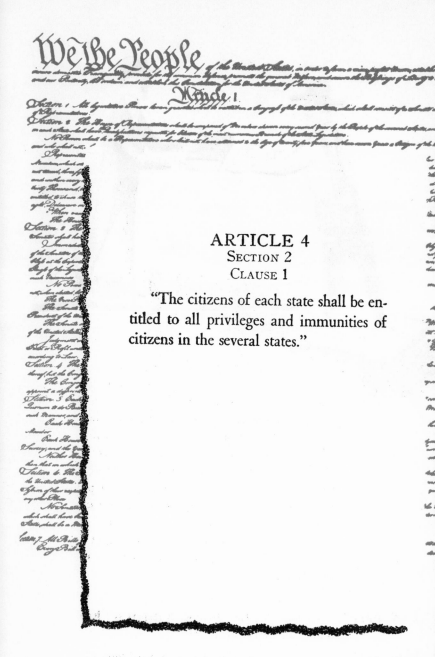

## ARTICLE 4
### SECTION 2
### CLAUSE 1

"The citizens of each state shall be entitled to all privileges and immunities of citizens in the several states."

This clause makes you realize that you are a citizen of the nation as well as of your own state. It means that you may go freely from one state to another and be treated about like everyone else. You may buy or sell property, get married, and pay taxes under the same rules as all other citizens of your new state. There are only a few special rights, such as the right to vote in your new state, that you may not have until you become a citizen of that state.

*You give:* Orders that the states must be fair to the citizens of other states.

*You get:* (a) Protection against unfairness as you go from one state to another; (b) citizenship in a great nation as well as in your own state.

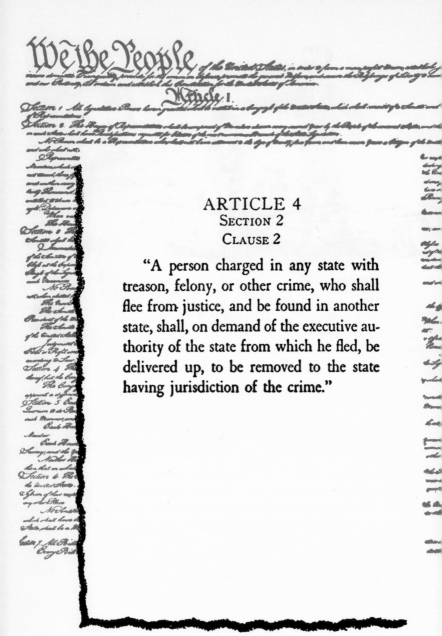

## ARTICLE 4
### SECTION 2
### CLAUSE 2

"A person charged in any state with treason, felony, or other crime, who shall flee from justice, and be found in another state, shall, on demand of the executive authority of the state from which he fled, be delivered up, to be removed to the state having jurisdiction of the crime."

Each state must arrest, try, and punish the persons who break its laws. Clause 2 keeps criminals from escaping punishment by running away to another state. It gives orders that criminals must be sent back to the states where their crimes were committed. This is called "extradition."

According to this clause, the executive authority (that is, the Governor) "shall" return the criminal to the state where he committed his crime. "Shall," however, has come to mean "may." In other words, a Governor cannot be forced to turn over a criminal if he sees good reason not to. In practice, however, a person accused or convicted of a crime is nearly always sent back, if caught, to the state where the crime was committed.

*You give:* Instructions for dealing with runaway criminals.

*You get:* Assurance that criminals cannot escape from the laws of one state by going to another state.

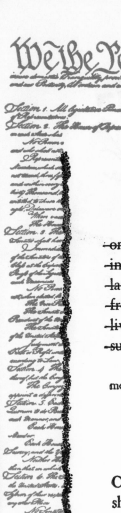

## ARTICLE 4
### SECTION 2
### CLAUSE 3

~~"No person held to service or labor in one state, under the laws thereof, escaping into another, shall, in consequence of any law or regulation therein, be discharged from such service or labor, but shall be delivered up on claim of the party to whom such service or labor may be due."~~*

* This clause referred to runaway slaves. Amendment 13 made it meaningless. (See page 226.)

### SECTION 3
### CLAUSE 1

"New states may be admitted by the Congress into this Union; but no new state shall be formed or erected within the jurisdiction of any other state, nor any state be formed by the junction of two or more states, or parts of states, without the consent of the Legislatures of the states concerned as well as of the Congress."

The first part of Clause 1 of Section 3 gave Congress the power to add to the Union all the states except the original thirteen. The clause also gives the rules for forming new states from the present states. The people of California could split their state into two states only if both Congress and the California Legislature agreed. Or, if the people of southern California wanted to unite their part of the state with a part of Arizona, they would have to get permission from Congress and the Legislatures of California and Arizona.

*You give:* (a) The right to Congress to admit new states to the Union; (b) instructions that protect the states from losing their lands.

*You get:* (a) A means by which the nation may grow; (b) protection from groups which might set up new states for selfish reasons.

# ARTICLE 4
## SECTION 3
### CLAUSE 2

"The Congress shall have power to dispose of and make all needful rules and regulations respecting the territory or other property belonging to the United States; and nothing in this Constitution shall be so construed as to prejudice any claims of the United States, or of any particular state."

This clause gives Congress the power to govern new territories added to the nation. Congress used this power in governing the Northwest Territory, the Louisiana Purchase, and other territories. Such government ended when the people living in those territories formed states which were added to the Union.

This same clause also gives Congress the right to set aside and care for national parks and forests, to improve public lands, to build hydroelectric projects like the great Hoover Dam, and in other ways to manage public property for the use of the people. (See page 91.)

*You give:* To Congress the right to govern the territories and make rules for the use of other property of the United States government.

*You get:* (*a*) Government for territories; (*b*) protection of public property by the members you elect to Congress; (*c*) improvement of parks, forests, deserts, and other property for the use of all the people.

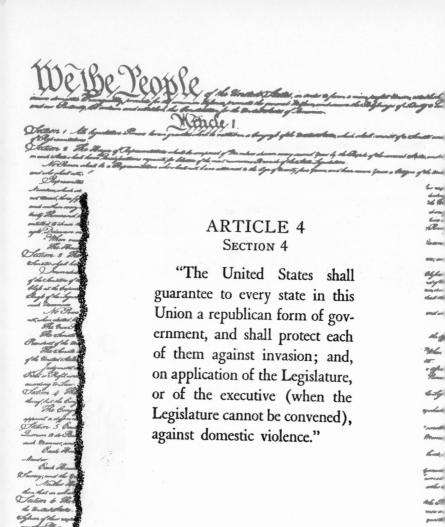

## ARTICLE 4
### Section 4

"The United States shall guarantee to every state in this Union a republican form of government, and shall protect each of them against invasion; and, on application of the Legislature, or of the executive (when the Legislature cannot be convened), against domestic violence."

The United States government guarantees to each of the states:

1. A "republican form of government."
2. Protection against invasion.
3. Protection, when needed, against riots or other disturbances within the state.

STATE GOVERNMENTS

FEDERAL GOVERNMENT

PEOPLE'S POWER HOUSE

This clause outlines duties which the federal government promises to carry out for the states.

The Constitution does not say what "a republican form of government" is, but most people agree that in such a government these things are true: (1) The people alone have the power to make and run the government. (2) The elected representatives of the people make the laws. (3) The powers of the government are explained and limited by a written constitution.

Suppose that a state should adopt a government that did not obey those three principles. Then it would be the duty of the United States government to step in and set up a republican form of government in the state again.

*You give:* The responsibility to your federal government to protect the political rights, the property, and the lives of the people in all the states.

*You get:* (*a*) Assurance that your state will not be turned into a dictatorship; (*b*) the whole force of the federal government to protect your state against invasion or against dangerous riots and other serious local troubles.

# ARTICLE
## 5

## THE MAKING OF AMENDMENTS

How Changes in the Constitution Are
Proposed and Adopted

## ARTICLE 5

"The Congress, whenever two-thirds of both houses shall deem it necessary, shall propose amendments to this Constitution, or, on the application of the Legislatures of two-thirds of the several states, shall call a convention for proposing amendments, which, in either case, shall be valid to all intents and purposes, as part of this Constitution, when ratified by the Legislatures of three-fourths of the several states, or by conventions in three-fourths thereof, as the one or the other mode of ratification may be proposed by the Congress, provided that ~~no amendment which may be made prior to the year one thousand eight hundred and eight shall in any manner affect the first and fourth clauses in the Ninth Section of the First Article, and that~~ no state, without its consent, shall be deprived of its equal suffrage in the Senate."

All through the summer of 1787, the delegates to the Constitutional Convention worked hard to finish the plans for the new government of the nation. When their work was nearly done, they felt that their plans would allow the citizens of the United States to live in peace. Each citizen could enjoy his own rights while also respecting the rights of others.

And yet, the wise men who wrote the Constitution were not entirely satisfied with it, and were not sure that they had thought of everything. They realized that, as the nation grew, future citizens would have problems quite different from their own. For these reasons, they wrote Article 5. Because of Article 5, changes in the Constitution can be made when necessary. The next few pages explain how such changes, called amendments, are made.

There are two main steps that must be taken to amend the Constitution. These are, first, the proposal of the amendment and, second, approval by the states.

Amendments may be proposed in two ways: (1) by a two-thirds vote in both the Senate and the House of Representatives; (2) in a national convention called by Congress when asked to do so by the Legislatures of two-thirds of the states.

Approval by the states of an amendment, called ratification, may also be obtained in two ways: (1) by the Legislatures of the states; (2) by special conventions called in the states. Congress decides which method of ratification shall be used. If three-fourths of the states approve the amendment, by either method, it becomes a part of the Constitution and a law for all the states.

## AMENDMENTS ARE PROPOSED
## BY

TWO-THIRDS OF EACH
HOUSE OF CONGRESS

OR

NATIONAL CONVENTIONS
CALLED BY CONGRESS

So far, all twenty-two amendments have been proposed in Congress. It is unlikely that an amendment will ever be proposed by a national convention. By the time two-thirds of the state Legislatures could ask Congress to call a convention for proposing an amendment, Congress would probably have proposed the amendment already. When Congress, not the Legislatures, proposes an amendment, much time, trouble, and expense are saved.

All amendments except Amendment 21 were ratified by state Legislatures. If all the states were to hold special conventions to ratify an amendment, the voters would have a better chance to show their wishes than they do when the Legislatures ratify that amendment. But such conventions would be much more costly than the method which has been commonly used.

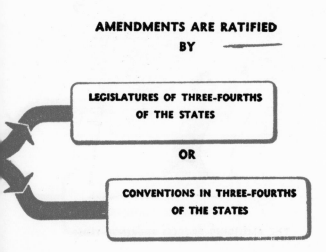

**AMENDMENTS ARE RATIFIED**

**BY**

**LEGISLATURES OF THREE-FOURTHS OF THE STATES**

**OR**

**CONVENTIONS IN THREE-FOURTHS OF THE STATES**

YOUR HOUSE OF FREEDOM

**THE AMENDING PROCESS PREVENTS THIS!**

Article 5, by which the Constitution sets up ways to change the Constitution itself, is one of the most important ideas included in our American form of government. When enough of the people in the nation want to make a change in the government, they may do so in an orderly way. The people may vote for representatives, both in Congress and in their state Legislatures, who will carry out the change.

In the United States it is not necessary for the people to use revolution and bloodshed to change the government. You may sometimes hear of groups of people "going underground"—that is, acting secretly against the government—or "plotting to overthrow the government of the United States."

When you hear about such groups, you should be suspicious of them. These people may be unwilling to follow the rules for changing the government which are outlined in the Constitution.

It is not easy to amend the Constitution. The men who wrote it had good reasons for making it hard to change. With their thorough knowledge of government and their practical experience, they wrote what they hoped was a sound and lasting Constitution. Yet they knew that changes in the country might make changes in its government necessary. They wanted the people to be able to change the plan—but only after a very large majority of the people had agreed that changes were necessary.

Since 1788, when the Constitution was adopted, many amendments have been suggested and talked over. But only twenty-seven amendments have been officially proposed and only twenty-two have been adopted. This small number of changes in more than one hundred and sixty years shows how wisely the men at the Constitutional Convention did their work. They put in the most important rules and ideas that would be needed in a strong Constitution; but they did not put in many little details. If they had, many of these details would have had to be changed later. As a result, our nation might not have been so strong as it is today.

Because it is not easy to change the Constitution, foolish or dangerous amendments are not likely to be accepted. The people must think carefully about every amendment that is suggested. They argue about it on street corners, in the newspapers, and over the radio. After studying what the people say, Congress plans an amendment carefully and then votes on whether or not to propose it. If an amendment is proposed, the state Legislatures vote on whether or not to add it to the Constitution.

Article 5 concludes "that no state, without its consent, shall be deprived of its equal suffrage in the Senate." This means that every state, no matter how large or small its population, shall always be allowed to have two Senators in Congress, according to Article 1, Section 3. The states with small populations had insisted on this right. Here in Article 5 they insisted again that, unless a state gave permission, no amendment should ever be made that would take away its right to two Senators.

*You give:* Permission for the Constitution to be changed, but only through the federal and state governments' working together.

*You get:* (*a*) A means by which amendments can be made when they become necessary or desirable; (*b*) assurance that the Constitution will be changed only when a very large majority of the people want the change.

# ARTICLE
# 6

## THE SUPREMACY OF THE CONSTITUTION

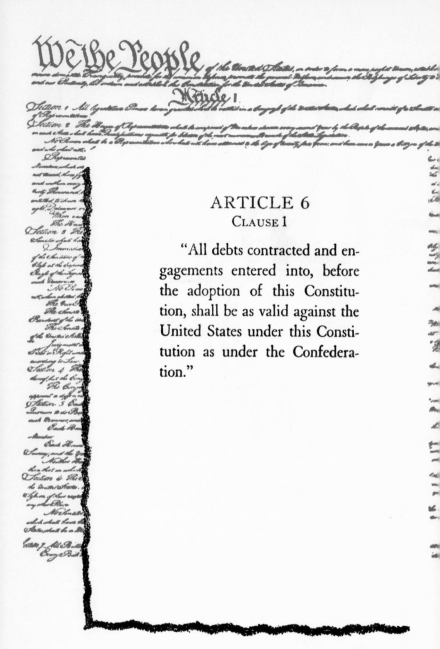

## ARTICLE 6
### Clause 1

"All debts contracted and engagements entered into, before the adoption of this Constitution, shall be as valid against the United States under this Constitution as under the Confederation."

In other countries, new governments had sometimes refused to pay back money borrowed by old governments. This clause said that our new government intended to pay back money borrowed by the earlier government under the Articles of Confederation.

When the new government began, it owed more than $50,000,000, but the bonds for this debt were actually worth only about one-fourth as much. Alexander Hamilton, first Secretary of the Treasury, got Congress to agree not only to pay off this debt at its full value, but also to pay back the money borrowed by the states during the War for Independence.

This honest way of paying debts, begun in the 1790's, has continued ever since. It is partly for this reason that our government has always found it easy to borrow money from its people at low rates of interest.

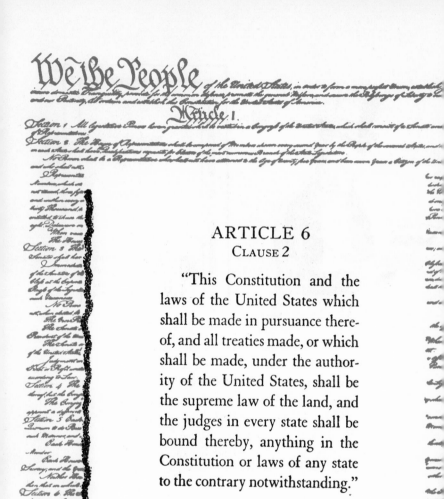

## ARTICLE 6
### CLAUSE 2

"This Constitution and the laws of the United States which shall be made in pursuance thereof, and all treaties made, or which shall be made, under the authority of the United States, shall be the supreme law of the land, and the judges in every state shall be bound thereby, anything in the Constitution or laws of any state to the contrary notwithstanding."

The Constitution speaks of only two kinds of government—federal and state—to which the people have given certain powers. State governments, however, have given up part of their powers to local governments—in counties, towns, and cities. Thus, in practice, we have three levels of government, each with certain powers.

When the powers of government are split up in this way, local laws sometimes disagree with state laws, and state laws with federal laws. Then there has to be some way of deciding which group of laws should be obeyed. Clause 2 of Article 6 directs that the Constitution, the treaties, and the laws of the United States shall be obeyed instead of state and local laws, whenever the laws disagree.

**DER OF LAWS**
**IN**
**UNITED STATES**

1. The Constitution of the United States
2. Laws and treaties of the federal government
3. Constitutions of the states
4. Laws passed by the states
5. Laws passed by county, town, and city governments

*You give:* Orders that the Constitution, treaties, and laws of the United States shall be supreme—that is, shall be above state and local laws.

*You get:* A firm Union that cannot easily be destroyed by quarrels as to whether the federal government or the state and local governments should have certain powers.

## ARTICLE 6
### Clause 3

"The Senators and Representatives before mentioned, and the members of the
several state Legislatures, and all executive
and judicial officers, both of the United
States and of the several states, shall be
bound by oath or affirmation to support
this Constitution; but no religious test
shall ever be required as a qualification to
any office or public trust under the United
States."

"I do solemnly swear that I will support and defend the Constitution of the United States against all enemies, foreign or domestic; that I will bear true faith and allegiance to the same . . ."

Cabinet Member

This clause was written to make very sure that all federal and state officials would know it was their duty to support and guard the Constitution. Without the Constitution to protect us, we, the citizens, might soon lose many or all of our rights and liberties.

The men who wrote the Constitution believed that religion and government should be kept separate. The last words of this clause, therefore, rule that nobody shall be kept from becoming an official of the federal government because of his religion.

*You give:* Instructions requiring every official of the federal and state governments to swear that he will uphold the Constitution.

*You get:* The solemn assurance of your government officials that they will be loyal to the trust you place in them.

# ARTICLE
# 7

*" The ratification of the Conventions of nine states shall be sufficient for the establishment of this Constitution between the states so ratifying the same."*

## THE RATIFICATION
## OF THE CONSTITUTION

How the Constitution Was to Be Adopted,
Along with the Signatures to the Constitution

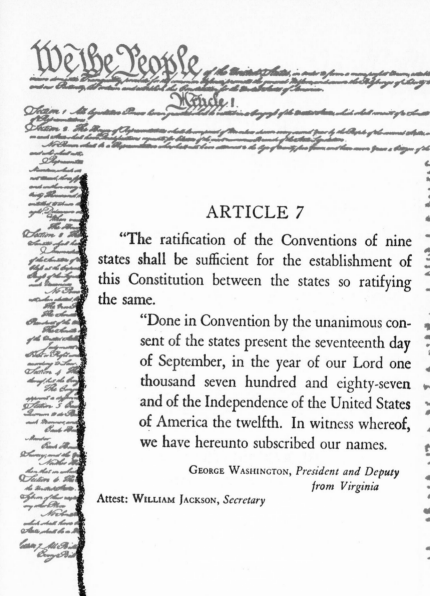

## ARTICLE 7

"The ratification of the Conventions of nine states shall be sufficient for the establishment of this Constitution between the states so ratifying the same.

"Done in Convention by the unanimous consent of the states present the seventeenth day of September, in the year of our Lord one thousand seven hundred and eighty-seven and of the Independence of the United States of America the twelfth. In witness whereof, we have hereunto subscribed our names.

GEORGE WASHINGTON, *President and Deputy from Virginia*

Attest: WILLIAM JACKSON, *Secretary*

NEW HAMPSHIRE
John Langdon
Nicholas Gilman

MASSACHUSETTS
Nathaniel Gorham
Rufus King

CONNECTICUT
William Samuel Johnson
Roger Sherman

NEW YORK
Alexander Hamilton

NEW JERSEY
William Livingston
David Brearley
William Paterson
Jonathan Dayton

PENNSYLVANIA
Benjamin Franklin
Thomas Mifflin
Robert Morris
George Clymer
Thomas Fitzsimons
Jared Ingersoll
James Wilson
Gouverneur Morris

DELAWARE
George Read
Gunning Bedford, Jr.
John Dickinson
Richard Bassett
Jacob Broom

MARYLAND
James McHenry
Dan of St. Thomas Jennifer
Daniel Carroll

VIRGINIA
John Blair
James Madison, Jr.

NORTH CAROLINA
William Blount
Richard Dobbs Spaight
Hugh Williamson

SOUTH CAROLINA
John Rutledge
Charles Cotesworth Pinckney
Charles Pinckney
Pierce Butler

GEORGIA
William Few
Abraham Baldwin

(NOTE: Rhode Island sent no delegate to the Constitutional Convention.)

DISCUSSION OF CONSTITUTION

After the Constitutional Convention, the Constitution was sent to Congress. In the debate which followed, John Adams said, "Our people must be consulted, invited to erect the whole building with their own hands, upon the broadest foundations." Adams wanted to be sure that the nation's government would be built to suit the wishes of the people.

In September 1787, Congress sent copies of the Constitution to the thirteen states for ratification. Within a year, eleven states ratified the famous document, making it the supreme law of the land.

George Washington became the first President in 1789. Before the summer of 1790, all thirteen states had ratified the Constitution. As members of a strong Union they had promised to build a new government for all the nation's citizens.

But there were many people who feared the new government and said that the Constitution should have more rules protecting the citizens. The First Congress, therefore, proposed twelve amendments to the states for ratification. Ten of these, called the Bill of Rights, were ratified in 1791. All the states have included similar bills of rights in their own constitutions.

ELECTION OF DELEGATES
TO STATE CONVENTION

STATE CONVENTION
ON RATIFICATION OF
THE CONSTITUTION

# AMENDMENTS TO THE CONSTITUTION
## I - IO

### THE BILL OF RIGHTS

### Adopted in 1791

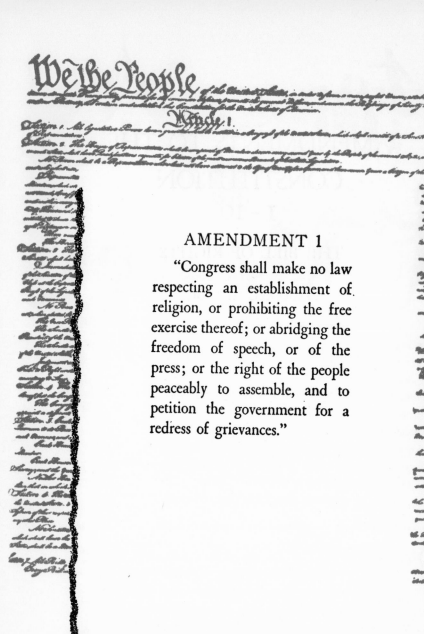

## AMENDMENT 1

"Congress shall make no law respecting an establishment of religion, or prohibiting the free exercise thereof; or abridging the freedom of speech, or of the press; or the right of the people peaceably to assemble, and to petition the government for a redress of grievances."

This amendment has these four important safeguards for the American people: (1) Congress must not set up any religion for the nation. It must not keep you from practicing whatever religion you prefer. (2) Congress cannot stop you from saying, writing, or printing almost anything you like. (3) Congress cannot keep you from meeting peaceably with other people to talk about anything you like. (4) Congress cannot keep you from asking your government to correct something that you think is wrong.

*You deny:* To Congress any power to take away your right to your own religion, to say or print what you think, to meet with other people, or to go to the government with your complaints.

*You get:* Protection against having these four important human rights taken away by the federal government. In some foreign countries, you would not have such rights protected by law.

[ 197 ]

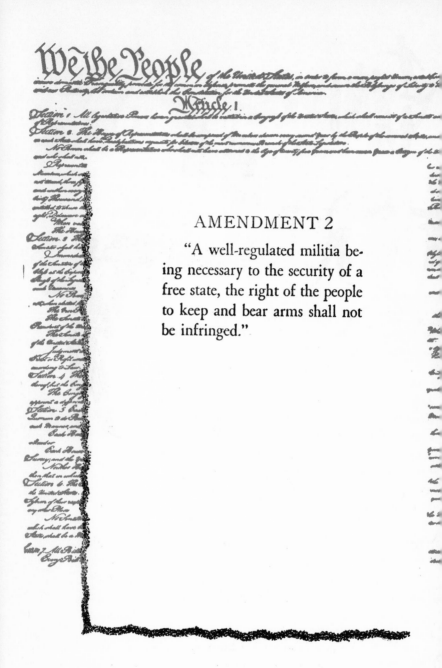

## AMENDMENT 2

"A well-regulated militia be-ing necessary to the security of a free state, the right of the people to keep and bear arms shall not be infringed."

A large national army sometimes puts freedom in danger. In some countries, army leaders have taken over the government and done away with the people's rights. Fearing such an army, our people wanted the right to have state militia, or citizen armies. (The National Guard in each state is made up of volunteers who are citizens.) This was the reason for Amendment 2. It keeps the federal government from passing rules forbidding the state militia to use arms in lawful ways.

*You deny:* To the federal government the power to interfere with your ownership and use of weapons for lawful purposes.

*You get:* Protection against the wrong use of power by a national army.

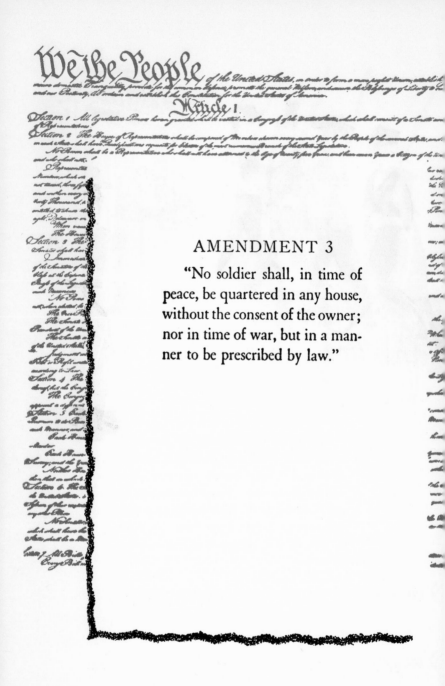

# AMENDMENT 3

"No soldier shall, in time of peace, be quartered in any house, without the consent of the owner; nor in time of war, but in a manner to be prescribed by law."

Before the Revolution, the British government often made the American colonists take soldiers into their homes and give them food and a place to sleep. The people bitterly resented this, and made up their minds that their new government should never have this right, even in time of war, except according to law.

*You deny:* To the federal government the right to place soldiers in your home unless a law allows the government to do so.

*You get:* Protection from having soldiers stay in your home against your wishes.

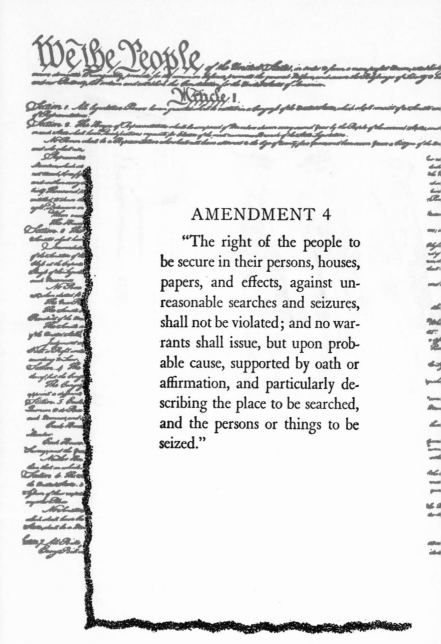

## AMENDMENT 4

"The right of the people to be secure in their persons, houses, papers, and effects, against unreasonable searches and seizures, shall not be violated; and no warrants shall issue, but upon probable cause, supported by oath or affirmation, and particularly describing the place to be searched, and the persons or things to be seized."

An old English law said that officers of the government must not arrest a person or search his home without the legal right to do so. But British officers in America had often broken this law. The people added this amendment to prevent such arrests and searches without a warrant from a judge. A warrant is a legal paper giving permission to arrest a person or search his home. A judge must not give out a warrant unless he is sure that there is good reason for it.

*You deny:* To any federal officer the right to arrest you or to search your home or other property unless he has a warrant to do so.

*You get:* Protection of your liberty and your privacy except when it seems probable that you have broken the law.

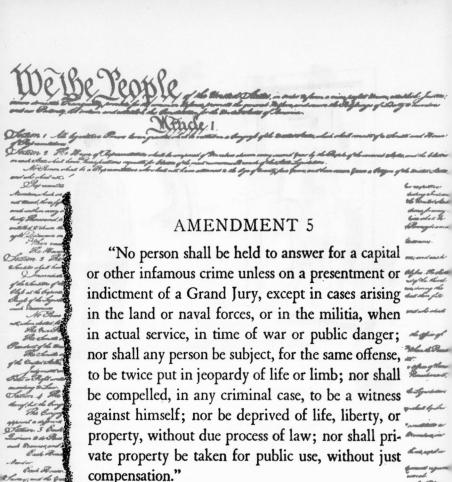

# AMENDMENT 5

"No person shall be held to answer for a capital or other infamous crime unless on a presentment or indictment of a Grand Jury, except in cases arising in the land or naval forces, or in the militia, when in actual service, in time of war or public danger; nor shall any person be subject, for the same offense, to be twice put in jeopardy of life or limb; nor shall be compelled, in any criminal case, to be a witness against himself; nor be deprived of life, liberty, or property, without due process of law; nor shall private property be taken for public use, without just compensation."

"I must warn you! Anything you say may be used against you!"

The first half of this amendment means this: The federal government cannot bring you to trial for a serious crime until a grand jury has decided that a crime has really been committed, and that you probably committed it. (Capital crimes are those which may be punished by death. Infamous crimes are those which may be punished by more than one year in prison.)

The rest of this amendment names certain other things that the federal government cannot do: (1) If you have been tried and found not guilty, the government cannot try you again for the same crime. (2) When you are being tried for a crime, the government cannot force you to say anything to injure yourself. (3) The government cannot execute or imprison you, or take away your property, except according to fair methods under the law. (4) If the government needs your property for some good reason, it must pay you a fair price for this property.

*You deny:* To the government certain powers over your life, your liberty, and your property.

*You get:* Protections that are very important to you as a free person.

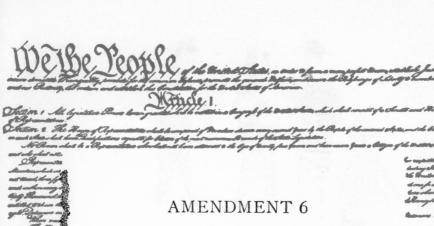

## AMENDMENT 6

"In all criminal prosecutions, the accused shall enjoy the right to a speedy and public trial, by an impartial jury of the state and district wherein the crime shall have been committed, which district shall have been previously ascertained by law, and to be informed of the nature and cause of the accusation; to be confronted with the witnesses against him; to have compulsory process for obtaining witnesses in his favor, and to have the assistance of counsel for his defense."

This amendment describes certain rights which the federal government must give you if you are arrested on a criminal charge. You must have: (1) a public trial as soon as possible after being arrested; (2) a jury of fair-minded citizens (usually twelve) who live near the place where you are supposed to have committed the crime; (3) information telling you just what you are supposed to have done, so that you can prepare your defense; (4) a chance to see, hear, and answer the witnesses who speak against you; (5) the help of the government, if necessary, in bringing to court witnesses who can help you; (6) a lawyer to defend you, paid for by the government if you are unable to pay him.

*You give:* Exact instructions to make sure that if you are accused of a federal crime you will have a fair trial.

*You get:* Protection against a trial by any method which might be unfair to you.

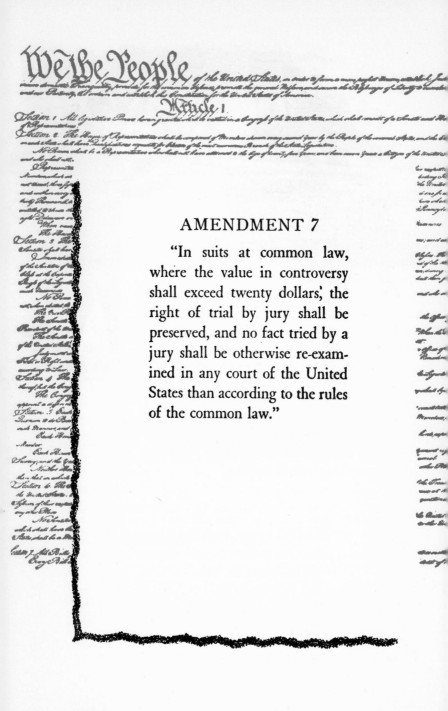

## AMENDMENT 7

"In suits at common law, where the value in controversy shall exceed twenty dollars, the right of trial by jury shall be preserved, and no fact tried by a jury shall be otherwise re-examined in any court of the United States than according to the rules of the common law."

"My client demands a trial by jury!"

Amendment 7 refers to cases of the kind usually called "civil suits." Such cases deal with disagreements about persons' rights and duties toward one another. When a civil case is tried in a federal court, the persons in the case may have a jury trial. But no jury is needed if the persons agree to do without one or if the money in the case is $20 or less.

When a case has been taken from a lower to a higher court, the judge or judges of the higher court may change the decision of the jury in the lower court only if (1) the exact meaning of the law was not understood correctly in the lower court; (2) the jury made its decision without hearing enough proofs of the facts.

*You give:* Instructions (*a*) that call for a jury trial in all civil cases except minor ones; (*b*) that tell the courts exactly how far they may go in questioning the work of the jury.

*You get:* (*a*) Protection against unfair decisions in civil cases; (*b*) respect for the decision of the jury; (*c*) the possibility of a different decision if the jury fails in its duty.

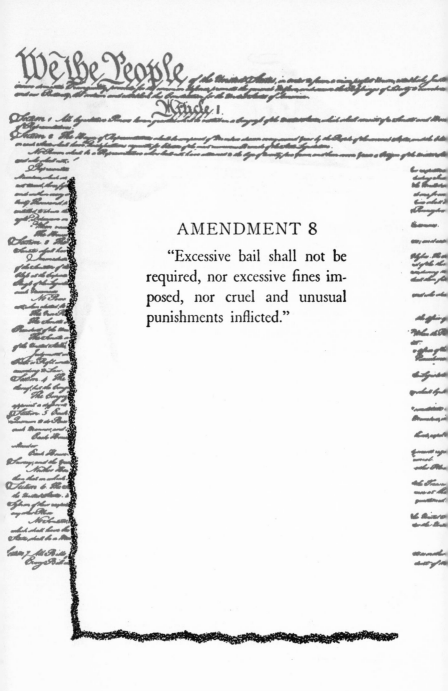

## AMENDMENT 8

"Excessive bail shall not be
required, nor excessive fines imposed, nor cruel and unusual
punishments inflicted."

After a person has been arrested, he is usually allowed to leave the jail until his trial. But before he leaves, he or someone else has to hand over money or other property to the court. This is called "bail." The bail is given back when the accused person comes to court to be tried. This amendment rules that federal judges must not ask for unfair amounts of bail. It also rules that people convicted of crime shall not be tortured, nor be fined or imprisoned more than is fair.

*You give:* Directions making sure that the courts will be fair, both to persons accused of crimes and to persons found guilty.

*You get:* Protection against being unfairly treated in the courts.

# AMENDMENT 9

"The enumeration in the Constitution of certain rights shall not be construed to deny or disparage others retained by the people."

The first eight amendments listed certain rights belonging to the people. Those rights were so clearly described that the federal government could make no mistake about them. It was not possible, however, to list all the rights which the people wanted to keep for themselves. Amendment 9 was added so that the federal government would not try to take away people's rights simply because those rights were not named in the Constitution.

*You deny:* To the federal government any control over rights not listed in the Constitution.

*You get:* (*a*) Protection against losing any rights that had not been put into the Constitution or the Bill of Rights; (*b*) another assurance that the people's power will not be taken away from them.

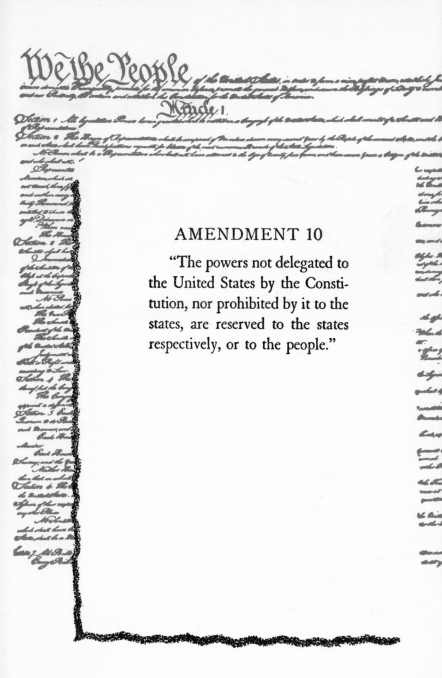

## AMENDMENT 10

"The powers not delegated to the United States by the Constitution, nor prohibited by it to the states, are reserved to the states respectively, or to the people."

UNDELEGATED POWERS OF THE PEOPLE

THE CONSTITUTION OF THE UNITED STATES

TO THE STATES

TO THE UNITED STATES

THIS AMENDMENT IS OF GREAT IMPORTANCE
TO <u>YOU</u>

"Powers not delegated . . . are reserved . . . to the people." Those words are of great importance. They were put into the Constitution because many leading Americans believed that *all* political power has always belonged to the people. As John Adams once said, "You have rights antecedent to all earthly governments; rights that cannot be repealed or restrained by human laws; rights derived from the Great Legislator of the Universe." Or, to say it in simpler words: The people have rights that come before the rights of the government. The people's rights come from God and cannot be taken away by human laws.

Each state had its own constitution which gave certain powers to the state government and kept other powers for the people. Under the Articles of Confederation, the states had given a few of their powers to the national government. But in the Constitution of the

United States, the people were assigning powers directly to the national government.

Amendment 10 was added to the Constitution because many people feared that the new national government might try to use powers it had not been given. This amendment made it clear that the federal government was to have only those powers given to it by the Constitution. Certain powers were to be kept by the states. All other powers were to be kept by the people. These powers kept by the people were not to be used at all unless the people decided to give them to the federal government by amending the Constitution.

State governments use their many powers to aid education, improve roads, furnish police protection, guard public health, and in other ways. The states give some of their powers for carrying out these duties to county, town, and city governments.

The constitutions of the states contain "bills of rights" much like the one in the national Constitution. Thus, the people have told their state governments exactly what powers they are trusting to the states and what powers they are keeping in their own hands.

Amendment 10 is the last amendment making up the Bill of Rights of our Constitution. These amendments name important safeguards for all citizens of the United States. In many other nations throughout the world there are millions of people who have no bills of rights to protect them. But the Constitution and its Bill of Rights helps all United States citizens to keep their rights to "life, liberty, and the pursuit of happiness."

# AMENDMENTS TO THE CONSTITUTION

## I I-22

## ADDITIONAL AMENDMENTS

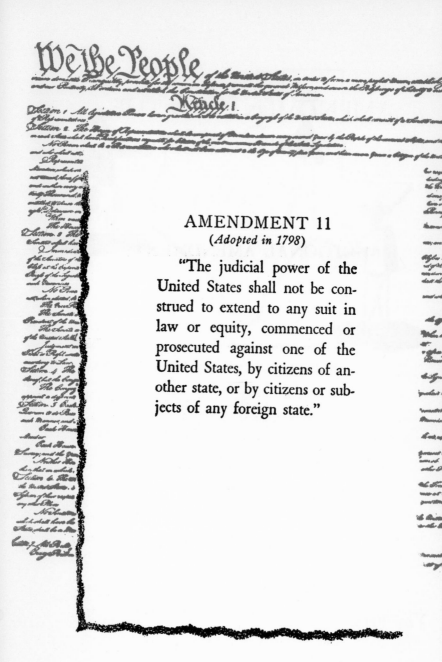

## AMENDMENT 11
### (*Adopted in 1798*)

"The judicial power of the United States shall not be construed to extend to any suit in law or equity, commenced or prosecuted against one of the United States, by citizens of another state, or by citizens or subjects of any foreign state."

This amendment was added to make clear the meaning of Article 3, Section 2, Clause 1 (page 146). That clause said that federal courts could try cases "between a state and citizens of another state." When approving the Constitution, the states thought this meant (1) that a state could bring a citizen of another state into a federal court, and (2) that no state could be brought without its consent into a federal court by a citizen of another state. When the Supreme Court ruled under Article 3 that a citizen of one state or of a foreign country could sue another state in a federal court, the states asked for Amendment 11.

*You give:* An explanation of the power of the federal courts to judge certain kinds of cases.

*You get:* Protection for a power of the states.

## AMENDMENT 12
### (*Adopted in 1804*)

"The electors shall meet in their respective states, and vote by ballot for President and Vice-President, one of whom, at least, shall not be an inhabitant of the same state with themselves; they shall name in their ballots the person voted for as President, and in distinct ballots the person voted for as Vice-President, and they shall make distinct lists of all persons voted for as President and of all persons voted for as Vice-President, and of the number of votes for each, which lists they shall sign and certify, and transmit, sealed, to the seat of the government of the United States, directed to the President of the Senate; the President of the Senate shall, in the presence of the Senate and House of Representatives, open all the certificates, and the votes shall then be counted. The person having the greatest number of votes for President shall be the President, if such number be a majority of the whole number of electors appointed; and if no person have such majority, then from the persons having the highest numbers, not exceeding three, on the list of those voted for as President, the House of

Amendment 12 changes Article 2, Section 1, Clause 3 (page 114). This amendment makes members of the Electoral College vote for a President and a Vice-President on separate ballots. The amendment became necessary after the election of 1800. By that time political parties had begun to select candidates. All electors of the Democratic-Republican party voted for Thomas Jefferson and Aaron Burr. This made a tie vote when the ballots were counted. Most of these electors wanted Jefferson for President and Burr for Vice-President. But when the tie vote was sent to the House of Representatives to be broken, the Federalist party very nearly voted to make Burr instead of Jefferson the President, against the wishes of the majority.

Article I

Representatives shall choose immediately, by ballot, the President. But in choosing the President, the votes shall be taken by states, the representation from each state having one vote; a quorum for this purpose shall consist of a member or members from two-thirds of the states, and a majority of all the states shall be necessary to a choice. And if the House of Representatives shall not choose a President, whenever the right of choice shall devolve upon them, before the fourth day of March next following, then the Vice-President shall act as President, as in case of the death or other constitutional disability of the President. The person having the greatest number of votes as Vice-President shall be the Vice-President, if such number be a majority of the whole number of electors appointed and if no person have a majority, then, from the two highest numbers on the list, the Senate shall choose the Vice-President; a quorum for the purpose shall consist of two-thirds of the whole number of Senators, and a majority of the whole number shall be necessary to a choice. But no person constitutionally ineligible to the office of President shall be eligible to that of Vice-President of the United States."

Because of Amendment 12 and the voting customs that grew up when political parties were formed, all members of the Electoral College now vote for a President and Vice-President exactly as the popular vote demands.

The Constitution did not say what should be done if a President was not chosen by Inauguration Day. Nor did it say that the Vice-President's qualifications should be the same as the President's. Amendment 12 made these and other points clearer.

*You give:* Orders that make sure there will be no more tie votes between President and Vice-President.

*You get:* (*a*) Greater assurance that the voters' choice will become President; (*b*) protection against a possible cause of bitter political quarrels.

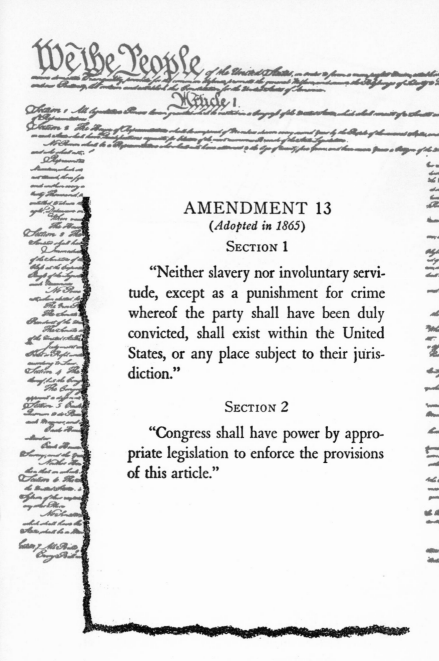

# AMENDMENT 13
*(Adopted in 1865)*

### SECTION 1

"Neither slavery nor involuntary servitude, except as a punishment for crime whereof the party shall have been duly convicted, shall exist within the United States, or any place subject to their jurisdiction."

### SECTION 2

"Congress shall have power by appropriate legislation to enforce the provisions of this article."

Amendments 13, 14, and 15 were added soon after the War Between the States. These amendments order the states not to do certain things, and give the federal government the power to make the states obey. These amendments also helped to settle an old disagreement about whether or not the states had a right to disobey the federal government. This disagreement had been one of the causes of the war.

Amendment 13 finally ended all slavery and "involuntary servitude" anywhere in the United States or its territories. Involuntary servitude is about the same as slavery. In general, Amendment 13 says that no one in the United States or its possessions may be made to work without pay or as a prisoner unless he has been found guilty of a crime and is being punished for it.

*You give:* (a) An order ending slavery; (b) power to Congress to make everyone obey the order.

*You get:* Protection against forced labor or imprisonment for all persons except criminals.

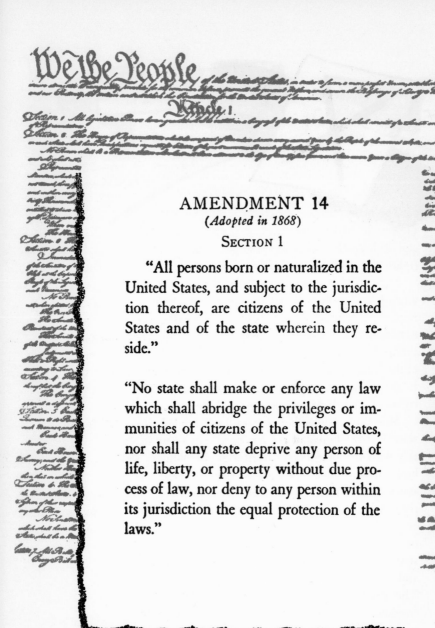

## AMENDMENT 14
### (*Adopted in 1868*)
#### SECTION 1

"All persons born or naturalized in the United States, and subject to the jurisdiction thereof, are citizens of the United States and of the state wherein they reside."

"No state shall make or enforce any law which shall abridge the privileges or immunities of citizens of the United States, nor shall any state deprive any person of life, liberty, or property without due process of law, nor deny to any person within its jurisdiction the equal protection of the laws."

The main purpose of Section 1, Amendment 14, was to make citizens of the former slaves and to keep the states from taking away their rights of citizenship.

Section 1 has a wider meaning than it had when it was written. It is now one of the most important parts of the Constitution. This section says that persons who were born or naturalized in the United States are citizens, both of the United States and of the state they live in. It also orders the states not to take away the rights of United States citizens.

Most important are the words: "nor shall any state deprive any person of life, liberty, or property without due process of law." These words have come to have these meanings: (1) The states must use fair, legal methods when they try to take away a person's life, liberty, or property. (For example, a man must not be beaten to make him confess to a crime.) (2) The states must not take away certain kinds of rights and privileges no matter how legally it is done. The words are used, for example, to protect freedom of speech, press, and assembly from interference by the states.

The last words of this section mean that whatever rights are given or rules are made, they must be the same for everyone.

# AMENDMENT 14
## SECTION 2

"Representatives shall be apportioned among the several states according to their respective numbers, counting the whole number of persons in each state, excluding Indians not taxed. But when the right to vote at any election for the choice of electors for President and Vice-President of the United States, Representatives in Congress, the executive and judicial officers of a state, or the members of the Legislature thereof, is denied to any of the male inhabitants of such state, being twenty-one years of age, and citizens of the United States, or in any way abridged, except for participation in rebellion, or other crime, the basis of representation therein shall be reduced in the proportion which the number of such male citizens shall bear to the whole number of male citizens twenty-one years of age in such state."

Before Amendment 14 was adopted, only three-fifths of the Negro slaves had been counted in the census. The purpose of the census was to find out how many Representatives each state might send to Congress (see page 20). But this amendment ruled that everyone was to be counted except Indians who did not have to pay taxes.

The Republicans knew that Amendment 14 would add to the number of Representatives from the Southern states, where the white population usually voted Democratic. The Republicans were afraid that they might lose some of their power in Congress unless the freed slaves, or freedmen, who were favorable to the Republican party, were allowed to vote. According to this amendment, if the white Southerners did not let the freedmen vote, their states would not be allowed to count those freedmen in their total population. Then the Southern states could not send as many Representatives to Congress as they could if they allowed their freedmen to vote.

# AMENDMENT 14
## Section 3

"No person shall be a Senator or Representative in Congress, or elector of President and Vice-President, or hold any office, civil or military, under the United States, or under any state, who, having previously taken an oath, as a member of Congress, or as an officer of the United States, or as a member of any state Legislature, or as an executive or judicial officer of any state, to support the Constitution of the United States, shall have engaged in insurrection or rebellion against the same, or given aid or comfort to the enemies thereof. But Congress may, by a vote of two-thirds of each house, remove such disability."

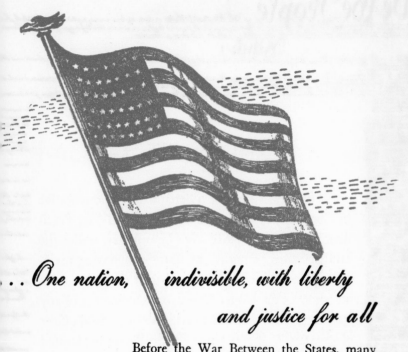

## .. One nation, indivisible, with liberty and justice for all

Before the War Between the States, many leaders of the Confederacy had been officials of the United States government or had held offices in state governments. When those leaders took office they swore oaths to support the Constitution. After the war, Congress decided that these men had broken their oaths when they joined or helped the Confederate forces. Congress, therefore, set out to punish these men by keeping them from holding public office again.

Because of Section 3 of Amendment 14, the Southern states lost many of their leaders. But in 1872 Congress ended this punishment for most of the men who had served the Confederacy. In 1898 all others were finally pardoned.

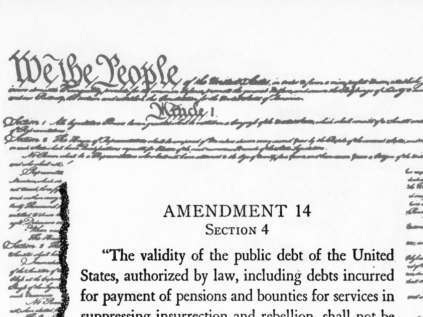

## AMENDMENT 14
### SECTION 4

"The validity of the public debt of the United States, authorized by law, including debts incurred for payment of pensions and bounties for services in suppressing insurrection and rebellion, shall not be questioned. But neither the United States nor any state shall assume or pay any debt or obligation incurred in aid of insurrection or rebellion against the United States, or any claim for the loss or emancipation of any slave; but all such debts, obligations, and claims shall be held illegal and void."

### SECTION 5

"The Congress shall have power to enforce, by appropriate legislation, the provisions of this article."

The first part of Section 4 was added so that Congressmen from the Southern states would not try to pass laws to keep the United States government from paying back the money it had borrowed during the War Between the States. The second part made certain that neither the federal government nor the state governments could pay back any money borrowed to help the Confederacy. Confederate bonds and money, of course, became worthless.

*You give:* (a) A clear description of United States citizenship and state citizenship; (b) instructions that keep the states from taking away certain important rights.

*You get:* Assurance (a) that all who should have citizenship will have it; (b) that if any state takes away certain important rights of citizens or others, the federal government will step in to protect them.

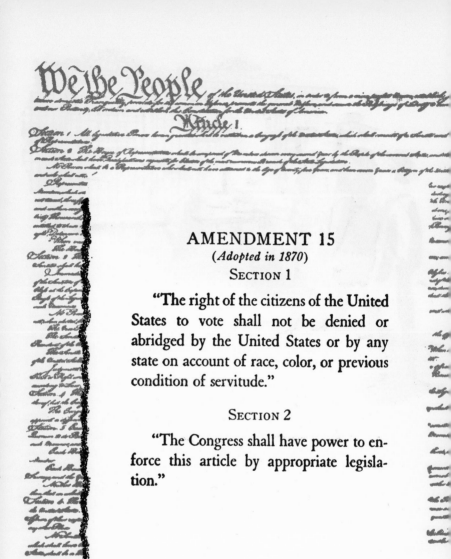

# AMENDMENT 15
### (*Adopted in 1870*)
#### SECTION 1

"The right of the citizens of the United States to vote shall not be denied or abridged by the United States or by any state on account of race, color, or previous condition of servitude."

#### SECTION 2

"The Congress shall have power to enforce this article by appropriate legislation."

This amendment ordered both the federal
and the state governments not to keep any citizens from voting because of race or color, or because they had once been slaves. Yet it did not
give all citizens the right to vote. The states
could obey the amendment and still be free to
decide which of their citizens should have this
right. Many states did not give women the
right to vote until 1920, when Amendment 19
was added to the Constitution (see page 245).
Yet Amendment 15 helped to strengthen the
people's control over their government.

*You deny:* To all governments within the United States
the right to keep anyone from voting because of
his color or race, or because of his having been
a slave.

*You get:* Assurance that fewer restrictions will be placed
on the right of citizens to vote.

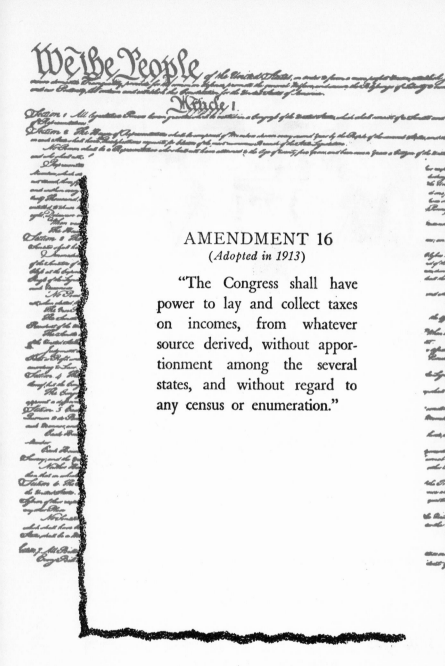

# AMENDMENT 16
*(Adopted in 1913)*

"The Congress shall have power to lay and collect taxes on incomes, from whatever source derived, without apportionment among the several states, and without regard to any census or enumeration."

Tax Collector

The Constitution gives Congress the power to collect taxes, but makes rules as to how this may be done (see pages 23, 64, and 98). One rule is that the amount of direct taxes taken from any state must depend on the number of people in that state.

In 1894 Congress passed a law taxing the incomes of the people in all the states. The following year the Supreme Court decided that this income tax law was unconstitutional. This law, the Court said, levied a direct tax in a way that did not take into account the number of people living in each state.

The federal government needed the money from the income tax to pay its growing expenses. For that reason, Amendment 16 was added to the Constitution. This amendment makes it constitutional for Congress to tax all kinds of incomes. The federal government now gets more of its money by taxing incomes than it gets in any other way.

*You give:* The federal government power to tax all incomes.

*You get:* Money to run the federal government.

[ 239 ]

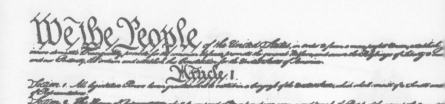

# AMENDMENT 17
### (*Adopted in 1913*)
#### CLAUSE 1

"The Senate of the United States shall be composed of two Senators from each state, elected by the people thereof, for six years; and each Senator shall have one vote. The electors in each state shall have the qualifications requisite for electors of the most numerous branch of the state Legislatures."

#### CLAUSE 2

"When vacancies happen in the representation of any state in the Senate, the executive authority of such state shall issue writs of election to fill such vacancies: *Provided*, That the Legislature of any state may empower the executive thereof to make temporary appointments until the people fill the vacancies by election as the Legislature may direct."

#### CLAUSE 3

"This amendment shall not be so construed as to affect the election or term of any Senator chosen before it becomes valid as part of the Constitution."

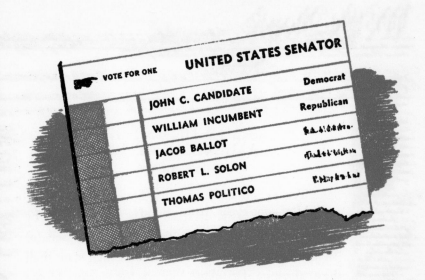

VOTE FOR ONE **UNITED STATES SENATOR**

| | | |
|---|---|---|
| | JOHN C. CANDIDATE | Democrat |
| | WILLIAM INCUMBENT | Republican |
| | JACOB BALLOT | |
| | ROBERT L. SOLON | |
| | THOMAS POLITICO | |

Before 1913, United States Senators were not elected by the voters; they were chosen by their state Legislatures (page 28). This method gave the voters little control over the Senate. Besides, the method did not work very well. For instance, some members of the Legislatures were suspected of taking bribes to choose certain men as Senators. It was finally decided that the voters should elect Senators just as they elect Representatives. Amendment 17 makes this the law of the nation.

*You give:* Instructions that Senators are to be elected directly by the voters.

*You get:* An elected Senate, which pays more attention to the wishes of the voters than did a Senate chosen by the Legislatures.

# AMENDMENT 18

*(Adopted in 1919)*

## SECTION 1

"After one year from the ratification of this article the manufacture, sale, or transportation of intoxicating liquors within, the importation thereof into, or the exportation thereof from the United States and all territory subject to the jurisdiction thereof for beverage purposes is hereby prohibited."

## SECTION 2

"The Congress and the several states shall have concurrent power to enforce this article by appropriate legislation."

## SECTION 3

"This article shall be inoperative unless it shall have been ratified as an amendment to the Constitution by the Legislatures of the several states, as provided in the Constitution, within seven years from the date of the submission hereof to the states by the Congress." *

* Amendment 18 was repealed by Amendment 21 (see page 250).

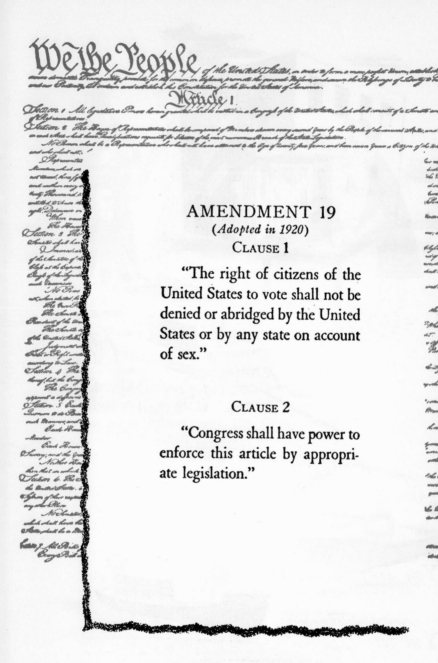

# AMENDMENT 19
### (*Adopted in 1920*)
#### CLAUSE 1

"The right of citizens of the United States to vote shall not be denied or abridged by the United States or by any state on account of sex."

#### CLAUSE 2

"Congress shall have power to enforce this article by appropriate legislation."

In the early years of our country, women had little chance to take part in government, and were not allowed to vote. During the 1800's, however, more and more women began demanding the right to vote. By the early 1900's, a number of Western states were already allowing women to vote. Finally, in 1920, Amendment 19 gave women in all parts of the United States the right to vote in state and national elections.

*You deny:* To the federal government and the state governments any right to keep citizens from voting because of their sex.

*You get:* The help of women in settling questions that affect all citizens.

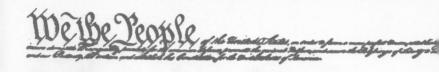

# AMENDMENT 20
### *(Adopted in 1933)*
## SECTION 1

"The terms of the President and Vice-President shall end at noon on the 20th day of January, and the terms of Senators and Representatives at noon on the 3d day of January, of the years in which such terms would have ended if this article had not been ratified; and the terms of their successors shall then begin."

## SECTION 2

"The Congress shall assemble at least once in every year, and such meeting shall begin at noon on the 3d day of January, unless they shall by law appoint a different day."

## SECTION 3

"If, at the time fixed for the beginning of the term of the President, the President-elect shall have died, the Vice-President-elect shall become President. If a President shall not have been chosen before the time fixed for the beginning of his term, or if the President-elect shall have failed to qualify, then the Vice-President-elect shall act as President until a President shall have qualified; and the Congress may by law provide for the case wherein

When the Constitution was written, it sometimes took weeks for people or mail to get from one part of the country to another. Because transportation and communication were so slow, the Constitution ordered that the new President and the new Congressmen elected in November should not begin their terms until the next March 4. This allowed them time to learn of their election and to get to Washington.

In later years such a long delay after the election was not necessary. It was also unwise, for two reasons: (1) After the voters had chosen the new President, they had to wait about four months before he could start doing the things they had elected him to do. (2) Even though the term of newly elected Congressmen began on March 4, they did not actually meet in Congress until the first Monday in December of the same year (see page 44). Unless the President called a special session of Congress, more than thirteen months went by before the Congressmen could start doing their work. From De-

neither a President-elect nor a Vice-President-elect shall have qualified, declaring who shall then act as President, or the manner in which one who is to act shall be selected, and such person shall act accordingly until a President or Vice-President shall have qualified."

## SECTION 4

"The Congress may by law provide for the case of the death of any of the persons from whom the House of Representatives may choose a President whenever the right of choice shall have devolved upon them, and for the case of the death of any of the persons from whom the Senate may choose a Vice-President whenever the right of choice shall have devolved upon them."

## SECTION 5

"Sections 1 and 2 shall take effect on the 15th day of October following the ratification of this article."

## SECTION 6

"This article shall be inoperative unless it shall have been ratified as an amendment to the Constitution by the Legislatures of three-fourths of the several states within seven years from the date of its submission."

cember of election year until March 4 of the following year, the old Congress could continue to sit.

In the old Congress there were some Senators and Representatives who had been defeated for re-election. Such members of Congress were called "lame ducks." If there were many "lame ducks," as sometimes happened, they could hold back important laws. Or the "lame ducks" could pass laws which the election had shown the voters did not want.

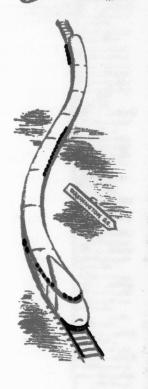

Amendment 20 is sometimes called "The Lame Duck Amendment." It orders the newly elected Congressmen to begin work on January 3, about a month and a half after election, and the new President to take office on January 20.

Amendment 20 also tells what shall be done if a newly elected President or Vice-President should die or for some other reason should not be able to take office. It also says what shall be done if a candidate dies while a close election is being settled in Congress.

*You give:* Instructions which (*a*) allow those you have elected to Congress to start carrying out your wishes soon after election; (*b*) prevent defeated members of Congress from staying in office longer than about a month and a half.

*You get:* A national government that is more likely to listen to the wishes of the people.

# AMENDMENT 21
*(Adopted in 1933)*

## Section 1

"The eighteenth article of amendment to the Constitution of the United States is hereby repealed."

## Section 2

"The transportation or importation into any state, territory, or possession of the United States for delivery or use therein of intoxicating liquors, in violation of the laws thereof, is hereby prohibited."

## Section 3

"This article shall be inoperative unless it shall have been ratified as an amendment to the Constitution by convention in the several states, as provided in the Constitution, within seven years from the date of the submission hereof to the states by the Congress."

Amendment 18, the Prohibition Amendment, made it unlawful to make or sell alcoholic liquors in the United States. That amendment was repealed by Amendment 21. Section 2 of the new amendment, however, protects any state that wants to keep prohibition.

# AMENDMENT 22
## (*Adopted in 1951*)
### SECTION 1

"No person shall be elected to the office of the President more than twice, and no person who has held the office of President, or acted as President, for more than two years of a term to which some other person was elected President shall be elected to the office of President more than once. But this Article shall not apply to any person holding the office of President when this Article was proposed by the Congress, and shall not prevent any person who may be holding the office of President, or acting as President, during the term within which this Article becomes operative from holding the office of President, or acting as President during the remainder of such term."

### SECTION 2

"This Article shall be inoperative unless it shall have been ratified as an amendment to the Constitution by the legislatures of three-fourths of the several States within seven years from the date of its submission to the States by Congress."

Glad to see you, Mr. President! As you know, this lease says you may not occupy the White House for more than two terms.

In 1940, when the United States was in danger of being drawn into World War II, Franklin D. Roosevelt was elected President for the third time. In 1944 he was elected again. Never before had a President been elected more than twice. If it had not been for the war, Roosevelt probably would not have been President for more than two terms. Many Americans have long believed that two terms are enough for a President.

After the war this belief was made a law. Amendment 22 keeps any President from being elected more than twice. It also keeps a Vice-President or anyone else from being elected to the Presidency more than once if he has already served more than two years to finish the term of another President.

# YOUR HOUSE OF FREEDOM

**YOUR HOUSE OF FREEDOM**

For more than one hundred and sixty years the United States of America has been a strong nation of free people. It is like a fine house, carefully planned, well built, and kept modern and in good repair. This house is so large and so carefully laid out that there is room in it for all who live here to work and enjoy life. The United States is truly your House of Freedom.

Before the Constitution was written, the American people tried for nearly six years to build a House of Freedom, using the Articles of Confederation as their plan. But the building they made showed many signs of weakness, and soon seemed likely to fall apart. It was as if each room in the house stood on its own foundation. Not until the Constitutional Convention did its work in 1787 did the American people understand how to build a House of Freedom that would be strong and lasting—the same one that we live in today.

The Constitution of the United States is like a plan, or blueprint, for your House of Freedom. The most important rules for the government of the country are written down in the Constitution, just as the right layout of the rooms is shown in the plan for a new house.

The government of the United States is like a building company chosen by the American people to help build the House of Freedom. There are three main branches in this company, each with its separate jobs to do.

The people elected by the voters to run the sawmills and cut the lumber for the framework of the House of Freedom make up the first, or legislative, branch of the government. These people are the Senators and Representatives in Congress, who make the laws for the nation.

The second, or executive, branch of the government is made up of the President of the United States and all the people who work with him. It is the President's job to see that the building goes up as the plan says it should. He is the builder in charge of construction.

President of the United States

CONSTITUTION AND BILL OF RIGHTS

GENERAL CONTRACTOR

Building inspectors make sure that the right kind of lumber comes from the sawmills and that the builder is following the plan carefully. In our government, this work is done by the third, or judicial, branch. It is made up of the Supreme Court and other courts of the United States.

As a citizen of the United States living in the House of Freedom, you enjoy precious rights which the Constitution guards for you. These rights were won for you by brave men of the past who believed in the goodness and intelligence of ordinary people. Perhaps you are so used to these rights that you take them for granted. But it is only in the United States and other countries with truly representative governments that the common people are protected against mistreatment by their fellow citizens or by their governments. You enjoy many rights that are denied to people in a large number of countries today.

These rights of yours are the same no matter what your race, religion, political beliefs, or wealth may be. Some of your rights are written in the Constitution or in the Bill of Rights and the other amendments. Other rights have become a part of our national laws and customs. These laws and customs may change, but your most precious rights as a citizen can never be taken away as long as you and other Americans understand and maintain the Constitution.

Some of the most important rights which the Constitution safeguards for you are shown on the following pages.

[ 263 ]

Among the important rights guarded by your Constitution are these:

The protection of a written Constitution which is the supreme law of the land (page 184).

A peaceful, lawful means of amending the Constitution (pages 171–79).

An energetic system of government capable of meeting your needs.

A system of checks and balances among the various departments of the government.

Protection against foreign invasion and domestic violence (page 168).

A republican form of government in your state (page 168).

Free movement among the states and the same privileges and immunities in all the states (page 160).

The right to vote regardless of race or sex (pages 236, 244).

The right to hold any public office for which you are qualified.

## PROTECT YOUR RIGHTS AS

# IN THE CONSTITUTION

✓ Freedom of religion, speech, press, assembly, and petition (page 196).

✓ Protection against unreasonable searches and seizures of your person or property (page 202).

✓ Just compensation for any property taken from you for public use (page 204).

✓ Protection against being deprived of your life, liberty, or property without due process of law (pages 204, 228).

✓ Freedom from slavery or involuntary servitude except as punishment for crime (page 226).

✓ Equal protection of the laws (page 228).

✓ Protection from bills of attainder and ex post facto laws (page 96).

✓ Protection against being held in jail indefinitely without a trial (page 94).

✓ Established procedures to protect your rights when you are accused of crime (pages 150, 204, 206).

✓ In criminal cases, the right to a speedy public trial by jury (page 150); in civil cases, a trial by jury if you want it (page 208).

# A UNITED STATES CITIZEN

Your Constitution is one of the best in the world. It was made rugged by earlier Americans. To keep it rugged is one of your first responsibilities.

But even the best constitution cannot guarantee that the government under it will be good. Since ours is a system of self-government, we have good government only when we, the people of the United States, play an active part in making it good.

The leaders of some foreign countries are enemies of our system of self-government. These leaders deny self-government to their own people and try to destroy it everywhere else in the world. There are even some enemies in our midst—people who would like to undermine our system of self-government and dictate to us what we should and should not do.

The duties of your American citizenship are powerful weapons against all such enemies. If you carry out the duties of your citizenship faithfully and to the best of your ability, the rights you cherish will be forever safe. No dictator will ever be able to seize your government, tear up your Constitution, and rule your life.

# EVERY TRUE AMERICAN

You as a true American can fulfill your responsibility for maintaining the Constitution and can help preserve it unimpaired for succeeding generations by carrying out these duties of citizenship:

Understand the principles of the Constitution, the greatest public document of the American people.

Stand up for the rights guaranteed you in the Constitution.

Vote in every election for which you are qualified.

Study the candidates and issues in each election, so that you may vote intelligently.

Keep informed about your government, so that you may use your vote and other rights of citizenship wisely.

Help create sound public opinion by taking part in public discussions, writing to your Congressmen about important issues, and in other ways.

Help in the work of the political party of your choice.

Seek public office when you feel you can be of service to your country.

# TO MAINTAIN AND PRESERVE

# HAS THE RESPONSIBILITY

✓ Serve willingly when you are called upon for jury duty.

✓ Pay your taxes honestly, realizing that the taxes you and other citizens pay are necessary to keep your government running.

✓ Watch the taxing practices of your government so that you can approve or disapprove them at election time.

✓ Be prepared to serve your country's armed forces.

✓ Don't seek unfair benefits from your government. Oppose anyone who does.

✓ Respect the laws of your community, state, and nation.

✓ If you disagree with the law, seek to change it through the regular processes of government.

✓ Be loyal to the principles of the Constitution and to the ideals of the American people as set forth in the Constitution.

# THE CONSTITUTION OF THE U.S.A.

# INDEX

## TO ARTICLES, SECTIONS, AND CLAUSES

# INDEX TO SUBJECTS

County governments: laws of, 185; powers assigned to, 217

Courthouses, owned by United States government, 91

Courts: and appointment of inferior officers, 130; federal, 82, 83, 144, 145, 147, 148, 208, 209, 220–21; and re-examination of facts, 208, 209; regular procedure of, 41

Credit: bills of, forbidden to states, 104; of the United States, 68

Crime: capital or other infamous, 204, 205; high, impeachment for, 140–41; in meaning of Constitution, 151; trial of, 150–51, 206, 207

Customs officials, appointment of, 133

Death, and succession to presidency, 120–21, 246, 248

Debts: incurred in aid of insurrection or rebellion, 234, 235; incurred under Articles of Confederation, 182–83; incurred in struggle for independence, 183; of an individual, 75; payment of, 64, 66, 104; validity of, affirmed, 182, 183, 234, 235

Defense, in trials, 206, 207; see also Common defense

Delegated powers: of federal government, 93, 216, 217; of state governments, 216, 217

Direct election, of Senators, 240, 241; see also Popular election

Direct tax: apportionment of, 20, 23, 65; on buildings or land, 99; on incomes, 99; on persons, 99; prohibited unless in proportion to census, 98–99

Discoveries, exclusive right to, 80–81

Disorderly behavior, 48

Disqualification, in cases of impeachment, 40

District courts, and federal cases, 149

District of Columbia: exclusive legislation over, 90–91; governed by board of commissioners, 91; as seat of government, 90–91

Division: of Congress into two houses, 17; of powers, 11, 15, 185; of Senators into three classes, 30

Dockyards, property of the United States, 90

Domestic tranquility, 7

Domestic violence, protection of states from, 168, 169

Draft, of citizens into the armed forces, 87

Due process of law, 204, 205, 228, 229

Duties: power to levy, 64, 65, 67, 72; restriction upon states to levy, 100, 106–7

"Elastic clause," 92–93

Election: campaign, 43; of Congress, 42–43, 46, 47; direct, see Direct election; popular, see Popular election; of President and Vice-President, 114–17, 222–25; of Representatives, 18, 19, 25; of Senators, 28, 240, 241

Electoral College, 115, 117, 223, 225

Electors: appointment of, 114; choice of, 115, 117, 118; and participation in rebellion, 232, 233; for President and Vice-President, 114–15, 117, 118, 222, 223; for Representatives, 18, 19; for Senators, 240

Emoluments, 52; from foreign powers, 102; beyond regular compensation, forbidden to President, 122

Enforcement: of amendments, 226, 234, 236, 242, 244; of laws, 12, 136, 138, 139

Enumeration: of certain rights in Constitution, 212, 213; power to tax without regard to, 238–39

Equity, 146

Evidence, inadequate, 209

Ex post facto laws: defined, 97; prohibited to national government, 96, 97; prohibited to states, 104

Excise, power to levy, 64, 65, 67

Execution of laws, 136, 138, 139

Executive authority, of state, 24, 30, 162, 168, 240

Executive branch, 11, 111–41

Executive departments. See Cabinet

Executive officers, and oath to support Constitution, 186, 187

Executive powers, vested in President, 112, 113, 128

Exemptions, of Congressmen, from arrest, 50

Expenditures, 102, 103

Export: duties on, prohibited to states, 106, 107; of intoxicating liquors, 242; of materials needed at home, 72; tax on, see Export tax

Export tax, on articles from any state, forbidden, 100, 101

Expulsion of Congressmen, 48

Extradition, 162–63

Facts: establishment of, 209; function of jury to decide, 151; re-examination of, 208, 209

Faith, interstate, 158–59
Federal courts. *See* Courts
Federal government: authority of, 90, 185; and Bill of Rights, 193; defined, 11; laws and treaties of, 185; powers of, 7, 8, 11, 12, 212, 213, 214–17; restrictions upon, 196, 217
Federal Reserve Board, appointment of members of, 133
Felonies: power to define and punish, 82; and privileges of members of Congress, 50
Fines, excessive, prohibited in Bill of Rights, 210, 211
First Congress, and Bill of Rights, 193
Foreign-born persons, and citizenship, 75; *see also* Naturalization
Foreign states: agreement with, 108; commerce with, 70, 71, 72, 93, 101, 107; disputes with, 83; and judicial power of United States, 146, 147, 220, 221; presents from, 102
Forests: owned by United States government, 91; power to regulate, 167
Forts, 90
Franklin, Benjamin, 5, 10
Freedom: of press, 196, 197; of religion, 196, 197; of speech, 196, 197
Fugitive, from justice, 162–63
Fugitive slaves, 164

General welfare: promotion of, 9; provision for, 64, 66
Gold and silver. *See* Coin
Good behavior, and terms of judges, 144
Goods: control over, entering or leaving country, 71; free flow of, 73
Government: based on separation of powers, 11, 15; characteristics of, 169; as federal system, 11; as landowner, 91; by the people, 3; and powers vested in, 92; republican form of, guaranteed states, 168, 169; seat of, 90, 91; three branches of, 11
Governor of state. *See* Executive authority
Grand Jury, indictment by, 204, 205
Grants, of states, 146
Great Britain, independence won from, 4
"Great Compromise," 21, 29
Grievances, right to petition for redress of, 196, 197
Guaranties to every state, 168–69

Habeas corpus, writ of, not to be suspended, 94–95

Hamilton, Alexander, first Secretary of the Treasury, 183
Hoover Dam, 167
House of Representatives: election to, 18, 19, 24, 42, 43, 46, 47; and election of President, 116, 222, 223, 224, 248; influence in, 23; legislative powers of, 14, 15, 56, 58; members of, *see* Representatives; officers of, 24, 26; organization of, 46–49; power of impeachment of, 24, 26, 27; qualifications for, 18, 46; representation in, 21, 22, 23, 29; and revenue bills, 55; vacancies in, 24

Immigration, control of, 71, 72
Immunities: of citizens, 160–61; of members of Congress, 50, 51
Impeachment: judgment of, 38–41; power of, 24, 26–27; of President, 38, 127, 140–41; removal of civil officers by, 140–41; for treason, bribery, and other high crimes, 140–41; trial of, 38, 39, 150
Import: of intoxicating liquors, 242, 250; of slaves, 94; of undesirable products, 72
Import duties: power to levy, 72; prohibited states, 106, 107
Imposts: forbidden states, 106, 107; power to levy, 65, 67
Inability of President to discharge duties, 120
Inauguration Day: choice of President before, 225; and oath of office, 125
Income tax, 99, 238–39
Independence, War for. *See* Revolution
Independence Hall, 5
Independence of the United States, 4, 190; debts incurred in struggle for, 183
Indians: citizenship of, 20; commerce with, 70, 73; protection of, from exploitation, 73
Indictment: of a grand jury, 204, 205; and impeachment, 40
Indirect taxes, 65, 67
Inferior courts, ordained and established by Congress, 82, 83, 144
Influence: Congressional, freedom of President from, 123; illegal, 141; undue, 53
Injustice prevented by Constitution, 6
Inspection laws, of states, 106, 107
Insurrection: debts incurred in, 234, 235; punishment of, 232, 233; suppression of, 88; *see also* Rebellion
Interest, on money lent, 69
International law. *See* Law of nations

Interstate commerce, 70, 71, 72–73, 93, 100, 101, 107; interference with, 73

Interstate Commerce Commission, appointment of members of, 133

Invasion: and power to call forth militia, 88, 89; and protection of states, 168, 169; and state action, 108; and suspension of writ of habeas corpus, 94–95

Inventors, and exclusive right to discoveries, 80–81

Involuntary servitude, abolished, 226, 227

Jail, 95

Jeopardy, twice put in, 204, 205

Journals of Congressional proceedings, 48, 49

Judges: and making of appointments, 134; federal, compensation of, 144–45; federal, tenure of, 144–45; and issuing of warrants, 203; of the Supreme Court, 130, 132; bound by supreme law, 184

Judgment: of elections, returns, and qualifications of members of each house, 46; of impeachment, 38–41

Judicial branch, 11, 143–55

Judicial officers, bound by oath to support Constitution, 186, 187

Judicial power: extent of, 146–47, 220–21; vested in Supreme Court and inferior courts, 144

Judicial review, 145, 149

Jurisdiction: appellate, see Appellate jurisdiction; over crime, 162; of federal courts, 147, 148, 220–21; of states, 164, 228; original, see Original jurisdiction

Jury: and re-examination of facts tried by, 208, 209; in suits at common law, 208, 209; trial by, 150, 151, 206, 207

Justice: established, 6; fleeing from, 162–63

King, and officers of the United States, 102

"Lame duck" amendment, 246–49

Land forces. See Armed forces

Lands, claimed under grants, 146

Law, 12, 15, 40, 41, 42, 50, 88, 102, 148, 158, 200, 228; on bankruptcies, 74, 75; common, see Common law; criminal, cases involving, 204–7; due process of, see Due process; equal protection of, 228, 229; and equity, cases in, 146; execution of, 88, 128, 136; incorrectly interpreted, 209; making of, 17, 22, 56–61, 169; necessary and proper, 92; order of,

184, 185; and order, obligation to maintain, 83

Law of nations, offenses against, 82, 83

Law of Presidential Succession, 121

Law of the land. See Supreme law

Legislation. See Law

Legislative branch, 11, 13–109

Legislative powers, vested in Congress, 14–17, 42, 64

Legislatures, state: and amending of Constitution, 172, 174, 175, 242, 248; and appointment of electors, 114, 115; and election of members of Congress, 18, 28, 42, 240; and formation of new states, 164–65; members of, bound by oath to support Constitution, 186, 187; and protection against domestic violence, 168, 169; and purchase of territory by Congress, 90; and vacancies in Senate, 30, 240, 241

Letters of marque and reprisal: power of Congress to grant, 84; prohibited states, 104

Libel, 51

Liberty, 229; and loyalty to Constitution, 187; protection of, 203, 204, 205, 228; secure blessings of, 10

Life, 7, 204, 205, 228, 229

Limb, jeopardy of, 204

Limited powers, 169, 214

Liquors, intoxicating: may be prohibited by states, 250; national prohibition of, 242; repeal of national prohibition of, 250

Louisiana Purchase, 167

Loyalty, to the Constitution, 187

Madison, James, 5, 10

Magazines, 90

Mail: routes for hauling, 79; system for handling, 79

Majority: in Congress, 46; and election of President and Vice-President, 116, 224; extraordinary, for amending Constitution, 178–79

Majority party, 25

Maritime jurisdiction, cases of, 146

Marque, letters of. See Letters of marque and reprisal

Measures, and weights. See Weights and measures

Measures, recommended by President, 136

Messages of President, 139

Military forces. See Armed forces

Military law, 87

President of the United States: compensation of, 122–23; election of, 114–17, 222–25, 252–53; executive power vested in, 112, 113; limitation to two terms, 252–53; oath of, 124–25; powers and duties of, 45, 56, 57, 60–63, 85, 91, 126–39; qualifications of, 118, 119, 246, 248; removal of, by impeachment, 38, 39, 120, 140–41; succession to office of, *see* Succession; term of, 112, 246

President pro tempore of Senate, 37, 121

Press, freedom of, 196, 197, 229

Prince, and officers of the United States, 102

Priority of supreme law, 185

Privacy, 203

Privileges: of citizens, 160–61, 228, 229; of copyright, 81; and loyalty to Constitution, 187; of members of Congress, 50, 51

Procedure, with bills, 54–63

Proceedings: journal of, 48; rules of, 48

Prohibition: of intoxicating liquors, 242, 250–51; of powers, 214–17

Property: private, 7, 202–5, 228, 229; of the United States, 90, 91, 166–67

Prosecutions, criminal, 206, 207

Public acts. *See* Acts

Public safety, 94

Punishment: for counterfeiting, 78, 79; cruel and unusual, prohibited, 210, 211; for disorderly behavior, 48; for impeachment, 40, 41; for insurrection of rebellion, 232, 233; of lawbreakers, 163; for treason, 154–55

Qualifications: judgment of, 46, 47; of the President, 118, 119, 246, 248; and religious test, 186, 187; of Representatives, 18, 19; of Senators, 32, 33

Quartering of soldiers, 200–201

Questioning: of Congressmen, 50; of validity of public debt, 234

Quorum, 46, 47, 116, 224

Race, and restriction of suffrage, 236, 237

Railroads, and interstate commerce, 73

Ratification: of amendments, 192, 193, 242, 248, 250; of Constitution, 189–92

Rebellion: 7; debts incurred in, 234, 235; payment for services in suppressing, 234, 235; punishment for, 232–33; and suspension of writ of habeas corpus, 94–95

Receipts and expenditures, regular statement of, 102

Recess of Senate, filling of vacancies during, 130

Recommendation of measures, power of President in, 136

Reconstruction amendment, 228–35

Records, interstate credit of, 158–59

Redress of grievances, 196, 197

Religion: freedom of, 196, 197; as test for office, 186, 187

Removal from office, by impeachment, 40, 41, 120, 140

Repeal of Amendment 18, 250–51

Representation, 20–23, 28, 29, 230, 231

Representatives: apportionment of, 20, 22, 29, 230; bound by oath to support Constitution, 186, 187; compensation of, 50, 51; death or resignation of, 25; election of, 18, 19, 25, 42, 43, 46, 241; and participation in rebellion, 232–33; privileges of, 50, 51; qualifications of, 18, 19, 46, 47; restrictions upon, 52, 53, 114; term of, 18, 19, 246

Reprieves and pardons, 126, 127, 128, 129

Reprisal, letters of. *See* Letters of marque and reprisal

Republican government: characteristics of, 169; guaranteed the states, 168, 169; steps toward, 237

Resolutions, approval of, by President, 62

Returns, 46, 47

Revenue: bills of, 54; equality of regulation of, 100; from taxes, 72

Revolution: American, 4, 7, 201; not necessary under Constitution, 177

Rights: of citizens, 159, 161, 193, 196–217, 228, 236–37, 244–45; reserved, 214–17; retained, 212–13; of states, 101

Riots, 169

Rivers, navigable, and interstate commerce, 72

Rules: for armed forces, 88, 89; concerning captures, 84, 85; governing territory and property, 166–67; of proceedings in Congress, 48, 49; uniform, for naturalization and bankruptcy, 74–75

Safeguards, 72, 145, 151, 217

Salaries. *See* Compensation

Science, promotion of, 80

Searches and seizures, 202–3

Secret ballots, 43

Secretary of State, 121

Securities, punishment for counterfeiting of, 78, 79

Seizures, and searches, 202–3

Senate, 28–41; and appointments, 130–35; and District of Columbia, 91; election to, 28, 42, 43, 46, 47, 240, 241; and election of President, 116; and election of Vice-President, 224, 248; equal suffrage in, 172, 179; and impeachment, 27, 38, 39, 41; officers of, 34, 35, 36, 37; organization of, 46–49; qualifications for, 32, 33, 46, 47; and revenue bills, 54; terms in, 28, 240; and treaties, 130, 131, 135; vacancies in, 25, 30, 240

Senators: apportionment of, 28, 29, 240; bound by oath to support Constitution, 186, 187; compensation of, 50, 51; division of, into classes, 30, 31; election of, 28, 42, 43, 46, 240, 241; and participation in rebellion, 232; privileges of, 50, 51; qualifications of, 32, 33, 46, 47; restrictions upon, 52, 53; term of, 28, 29, 240, 246

Separation: of powers, 11, 15, 185; of religion and government, 186, 187

Service of the United States, employment of militia in, 88, 89, 126

Servitude, and restriction of suffrage, 236, 237

Sessions of Congress, 45, 48; special, 45, 136, 139

Sex, and restriction of suffrage, 244, 245

Shipping: aids to, 72; equality of, 101

Ships of war prohibited to states, 108

Signers of the Constitution, 190–91

Silver. *See* Coin

Slander, 51

Slavery: abolished, 226–27; and citizenship, 229

Slaves, claims for loss of, 234; regulation of trade in, 94; return of runaway, 164

Soldiers, 200–201

Sovereign power, 11, 169

Speaker of the House, 24, 25, 26, 121

Special elections, of Representatives, 25

Speech, freedom of, 196, 197, 229

"Spoils System," 135

Standard of weights and measures, 76, 77

State Department, 131

State of the Union, 136, 139

Statement of receipts and expenditures, 102

States: under Articles of Confederation, 4, 5, 7, 11; and Bill of Rights, 193; and bills of rights in own constitutions, 193, 217; citizens of, 160–61, 228, 229, 236, 237, 244, 245; claims of, 166; and commerce, 70, 100–101; under Constitution, 5, 11, 12; and credit of public acts of other states, 158–59; debts incurred by, 183, 234; executive authority of, 24, 30, 162–63, 168, 240; governments of, 12, 217; grants of, 146, 147; guaranties to, 168–69; judicial power over, 146–48; and militia, 88; new, 164–65; officers of, 186, 187; powers of, 185, 214–17; and prohibition of intoxicating liquors, 250, 251; quarrels among the, 4, 7; and ratification of Constitution, 190; representation of, in Congress, 18, 20–23, 28, 172, 179; restrictions upon, 104–9, 228, 229; trials held in, 150

Succession to presidency, 25, 26, 120–21, 246, 248, 249

Suffrage: restrictions on abridgment of, 236–37, 244–45; in states, 172, 179

Suits: at common law, 208, 209; in law and equity, 146

Supreme Court: judges of, 130, 132, 144, 145; judicial power vested in, 144, 145; jurisdiction of, 148–49; rulings of, 93

Supreme law, 184, 192

Tariffs, 72, 107.

Tax: direct, *see* Direct tax; on exports, 100, 101; income, 99, 238, 239; power to levy, 64, 65, 67, 72

Telegraph, and interstate commerce, 73

Tender, in payment of debts, 104

Terms: of judges, 144, 145; of President, 112, 246, 247, 249, 252–53; of Representatives, 18, 246, 249; of Senators, 28, 240, 246, 249

Territory, 166–67, 250

Third term for President forbidden, 252–53

Title, of nobility, 102–4

Tonnage, duty of, forbidden states, 108, 109

Town governments: laws of, 185; powers assigned to, 217

Transportation, 71, 79

Treason: attainder of, 154, 155; conviction of, 152, 153; defined, 141, 152–53; impeachment of civil officers for, 140–41; punishment for, 154–55

Treasury: appropriations from, 50, 102, 103; and states, 106

Treaties: cases arising under, 146, 147; making and approval of, 128, 130, 131, 135; prohibited states, 104, 105; as supreme law, 184, 185

Trials, 150–51, 206–9

Tribunals. *See* Courts

Troops. *See* Armies

Tyranny, 6, 10, 153, 229

Unconstitutionality: of interference with interstate commerce, 73; of laws, power to declare, 145

Uniformity: of administration of justice, 145; of bankruptcy rules, 74, 75; of commerce regulations, 71, 72, 107; of naturalization rules, 74; of postage rates, 79; of taxes, 64, 67

Union: admission of new states to, 20, 164–65; a more perfect, 5, 6, 7; state of the, 136, 139

United Nations, 8

Vacancies: in House of Representatives, 24; occurring during recess of Senate, 130; in Senate, 30, 240

Validity, of United States debt, 182, 183, 234, 235

Value: in controversy, in suits at common law, 208, 209; of money, regulation of, 76, 77

Verdict: of jury, and establishment of fact, 209; may be changed, 209

Vessels, in interstate commerce, 100

Veto, 56, 57, 61, 63

Vice-President: in Cabinet, 35; compensation of, 123; as elected President, limitation on terms of, 252–53; election of, 114–17, 222–24; impeachment of, 140–41; as president of Senate, 34, 35, 36, 39; qualifications of, 224, 225, 246, 248; in succession to presidency, 113, 252–53; term of, 112, 246; voting rights of, in Senate, 34, 35

Voting: for adoption of Constitution, 192, 193; of electors, 114, 115, 116, 118, 222, 223; as right of citizens, 230, 231, 236, 237, 244, 245; rules of, 19, 161

War: begun by a foreign power, 85; power to declare, 84, 85; power to engage in, prohibited states, 108; and quartering of soldiers, 200, 201; time of, and crimes, 204; and treason, 152

War Between the States, 227; debts incurred during, 234, 235

Warrants, for search and seizure, 202, 203

Washington, D.C., 3. *See also* District of Columbia

Washington, George, first President, 5, 11, 192

Weights and measures, regulation of, 76, 77

Welfare, general, 9

Witness: compulsory process for obtaining, 206, 207; confrontation with, 206, 207; and conviction of treason, 152–53; no person compelled to act as, against himself, 204, 205

Women: vote denied to, 237, 245; suffrage extended to, 244, 245

World trade, 101

Writ of habeas corpus. *See* Habeas corpus.

Writings, exclusive right to, 80–81

Writs of election, 24

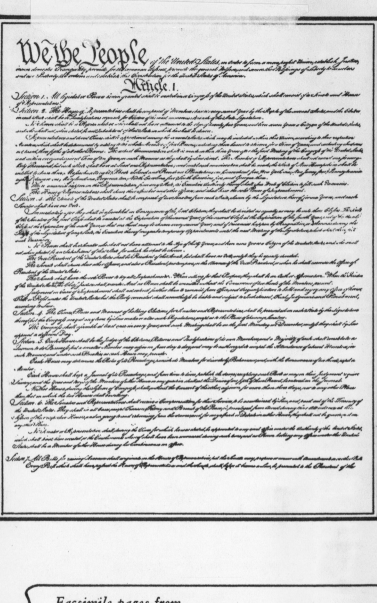